RWANDA

COUNTRY TORN APART

RWANDA

COUNTRY TORN APART

by Kari Bodnarchuk

Lerner Publications Company / Minneapolis

Lerner Publications Company
A Division of Lerner Publishing Group
241 First Avenue North
Minneapolis, MN 55401 U.S.A

Website address: www.lernerbooks.com

All maps by Philip Schwartberg, Meridian Mapping, Minneapolis.
Cover photo © Betty Press/Panos Pictures
Table of contents photos from top to bottom by United Nations Commission on Refugees; Editions L'Harmattan; Reuters/Corinne Dufka/Archive Photos; Reuters/Ulli Michel/Archive Photos; ©Kari Bodnarchuk

Series Consultant: Andrew Bell-Fialkoff
Editorial Director: Mary M. Rodgers
Editor: Chris Dall
Designer: Michael Tacheny
Photo Researcher: Cheryl L. Hulting

LIBRARY OF CONGRESS CATALOGING-IN-PUBLICATION DATA

Bodnarchuk, Kari.
    Rwanda : country torn apart / by Kari Bodnarchuk
      p.   cm. – (world in conflict)
    Includes bibliographical references and index.
    Summary: Describes the history of Rwanda's ethnic conflict between the Hutu and Tutsi tribes, and its continuing effect on the people of that country.
    ISBN 0-8225-3557-2 (lib. bdg : alk. paper)
    1. Rwanda—History—Civil War, 1994—Juvenile literature.
2. Genocide—Rwanda—Juvenile literature. 3. Rwanda—Ethnic relations—Juvenile literature. [1. Rwanda—History—Civil War, 1994. 2. Rwanda—Ethnic relations] I. Title. II. Series.
    DT450.435B563 2000
    967.571—dc20   96-43424

Manufactured in the United States of America
1 2 3 4 5 6 – JR – 05 04 03 02 01 00

CONTENTS

ABOUT THIS SERIES

Government firepower kills 25 protesters . . . . Thousands of refugees flee the country . . . . Rebels attack capital . . . . Racism and rage flare . . . . Fighting breaks out . . . . Peace talks stall . . . . Bombing toll rises to 52 . . . . Slaughter has cost up to 50,000 lives.

Conflicts between people occur across the globe, and we hear about some of the more spectacular and horrific episodes in the news. But since most fighting doesn't directly affect us, we often choose to ignore it. And even if we do take the time to learn about these conflicts—from newspapers, magazines, television news, or radio—we're often left with just a snapshot of the conflict instead of the whole reel of film.

Most news accounts don't tell you the whole story about a conflict, focusing instead on the attention-grabbing events that make the headlines. In addition, news sources may have a preconceived idea about who is right and who is wrong in a conflict. The stories that result often portray one side as the "bad guys" and the other as the "good guys."

The *World in Conflict* series approaches each conflict with the idea that wars and political disputes aren't simply about bullies and victims. Conflicts are complex problems that can often be traced back hundreds of years. The people fighting one another have complicated reasons for doing so. Fighting erupts between groups divided by ethnicity, religion, and nationalism. These groups fight over power, money, territory, control. Sometimes people who just want to go about their own business get caught up in a conflict just because they're there.

These books examine major conflicts around the world, some of which are very bloody and others that haven't involved a lot of violence. They portray the people involved in and affected by conflicts. They describe how each conflict got started, how it developed, and where it stands. The books also outline some of the ways people have tried to end the conflicts. By reading the stories behind the headlines, you will learn some reasons why people hate and fight one another and, in addition, why some people struggle so hard to end conflicts.

WORDS YOU NEED TO KNOW

Banyarwanda: A Kinyarwanda word meaning "the people of Rwanda." The term is most often used in reference to Tutsi exiles in Uganda, the Democratic Republic of the Congo, and Burundi.

coup d'état: French words meaning "blow to the state" that refer to a swift, sudden overthrow of a government.

ethnic group: A permanent group of people bound together by a combination of cultural markers, which may include—but are not limited to—race, nationality, tribe, religion, customs, and historical origins.

extremist: A person who advocates extreme political measures, such as the imprisonment or killing of political opponents.

feudal system: An economic relationship in which a landowner provides land to a peasant in return for services.

genocide: The systematic killing or harming of a national, ethnic, racial, or religious group with the intent of eliminating it.

militia group: A supplementary fighting force. Often, but not always, this term is used to describe underground, illegal groups. Sometimes an illegal militia group may support, through the use of violence, the current government and its policies. The aim of other militia groups is the overthrow of the government.

nongovernmental organization (NGO): A private organization that provides aid to people without being affiliated with any particular government. NGOs often provide medical and humanitarian assistance to war-torn regions. In postwar situations, NGOs concentrate on rebuilding and reconciliation.

prefecture: An administrative district.

propaganda: Ideas, rumors, or information spread to influence people's opinion. The intent of propaganda may be either to injure or to promote an institution, a cause, or a people.

FOREWORD

by Andrew Bell-Fialkoff

Conflicts between various groups are as old as time. Peoples and tribes around the world have fought one another for thousands of years. In fact our history is in great part a succession of wars—between the Greeks and the Persians, the English and the French, the Russians and the Poles, and many others. Not only do states or ethnic groups fight one another, so do followers of different religions—Catholics and Protestants in Northern Ireland, Christians and Muslims in Bosnia, and Buddhists and Hindus in Sri Lanka. Often ethnicity, language, and religion—some of the main distinguishing elements of culture—reinforce one another in characterizing a particular group. For instance, the vast majority of Greeks are Orthodox Christian and speak Greek; most Italians are Roman Catholic and speak Italian. Elsewhere, one cultural aspect predominates. Serbs and Croats speak dialects of the same language but remain separate from one another because most Croats are Catholics and most Serbs are Orthodox Christians. To those two groups, religion is more important than language in defining culture.

We have witnessed an increasing number of conflicts in modern times—why? Three reasons stand out. One is that large empires—such as Austria-Hungary, Ottoman Turkey, several colonial empires with vast holdings in Asia, Africa, and America, and, most recently, the Soviet Union—have collapsed. A look at world maps from 1900, 1950, and 1998 reveals an ever-increasing number of small and medium-sized states. While empires existed, their rulers suppressed many ethnic and religious conflicts. Empires imposed order, and local resentments were mostly directed at the central authority. Inside the borders of empires, populations were multiethnic and often highly mixed. When the empires fell apart, world leaders found it impossible to establish political frontiers that coincided with ethnic boundaries. Different groups often claimed territories inhabited by others. The nations created on the lands of a toppled empire were saddled with acute border and ethnic problems from their very beginnings.

The second reason for more conflicts in modern times stems from the twin ideals of freedom and equality. In the United States, we usually think of freedom as "individual freedom." If we all have equal rights, we are free. But if you are a member of a minority group and feel that you are being discriminated against, your group's rights and freedoms are also important to you. In fact, if you don't have your "group freedom," you don't have full individual freedom either.

After World War I (1914–1918), the allied western nations, under the guidance of U.S. president Woodrow Wilson, tried to satisfy group rights by promoting minority rights. The spread of frantic nationalism in the 1930s, especially among disaffected ethnic minorities, and the catastrophe of World War II (1939–1945) led to a fundamental reassessment of the Wilsonian philosophy. After 1945 group rights were downplayed on the assumption that guaranteeing individual rights would be sufficient. In later decades, the collapse of multiethnic nations like Czechoslovakia, Yugoslavia, and the Soviet Union—coupled with the spread of nationalism in those regions—came as a shock to world leaders. People want democracy and individual rights, but they want their group rights, too. In practice, this means more conflicts and a cycle of secession, as minority ethnic groups seek their own sovereignty and independence.

The fires of conflict are often further stoked by the media, which lavishes glory and attention on independence movements. To fight for freedom is an honor. For every Palestinian who has killed an Israeli, there are hundreds of Kashmiris, Tamils, and Bosnians eager to shoot at their enemies. Newspapers, television and radio news broadcasts, and other media play a vital part in fomenting that sense of honor. They magnify each crisis, glorify rebellion, and help to feed the fire of conflict.

The third factor behind increasing conflict in the world is the social and geographic mobility that modern society enjoys. We can move anywhere we want and can aspire—or so we believe—to be anything we wish. Every day the television tantalizingly dangles the prizes that life can offer. We all want our share. But increased mobility and ambition also mean increased competition, which leads to antagonism. Antagonism often fastens itself to ethnic, racial, or religious differences. If you are an inner-city African American and your local grocer happens to be Korean American, you may see that individual as different from yourself—an intruder—rather than as a person, a neighbor, or a grocer. This same feeling of "us" versus "them" has been part of many an ethnic conflict around the world.

Many conflicts have been contained—even solved—by wise, responsible leadership. But unfortunately, many politicians use citizens' discontent for their own ends. They incite hatred, manipulate voters, and mobilize people against their neighbors. The worst things happen when neighbor turns against neighbor. In Bosnia, in Rwanda, in Lebanon, and in countless other places, people who had lived and worked together and had even intermarried went on a rampage, killing, raping, and robbing one another with gusto. If the appalling carnage teaches us anything, it is that we should stop seeing one another as hostile competitors and enemies and accept one another as people. Most importantly, we should learn to understand why conflicts happen and how they can be prevented. That is why *World in Conflict* is so important—the books in this series will help you understand the history and inner dynamics of some of the most persistent conflicts of modern times. And understanding is the first step to prevention. ⊕

INTRODUCTION

The landlocked republic of Rwanda, located in the center of eastern Africa, is one of the most mountainous countries on the African continent. Although the country is known for its mountains, some of which reach 14,000 feet above sea level, Rwanda is a land of diversity. The terrain in the western region of Rwanda includes rain forests and volcanoes, as well as steep, sharp-edged mountains and terraced hillsides. Banana plantations and eucalyptus trees blanket rounded hills in the central region, while marshes, lakes, and grassy plains are characteristic of the country's eastern landscape.

This tiny nation, one of the smallest in Africa, covers about 10,000 square miles, which is roughly the size of the state of Maryland. With eight million people, however, Rwanda has about twice as many residents as Maryland. The Democratic Republic of the Congo (known as Zaire from 1971 to 1997) and sprawling Lake Kivu border Rwanda to the west. Uganda lies to the north, while Tanzania sits to the east and Burundi to the south. Because of the large and small lakes in this part of eastern Africa, the area is sometimes referred to as the Great Lakes Region.

Rwanda is divided into 10 districts, called **prefectures.** These prefectures include about 143 communes, which are the administrative divisions of the prefectures. This structure is similar to the one found in the United States, which is broken down into states and counties. Rwanda's only city is Kigali, the capital, which is located in central Rwanda and is the administrative center of the Kigali prefecture. The country's main towns are the administrative centers of the other nine prefectures. Some of the most important towns are Gisenyi, located on Lake Kivu, Butare in the south, and Ruhengeri in the northwest. Small, rural farms are found throughout the rest of the country.

Facing page: Although Rwanda is one of Africa's smallest nations, its recent troubles have brought it into the international spotlight.

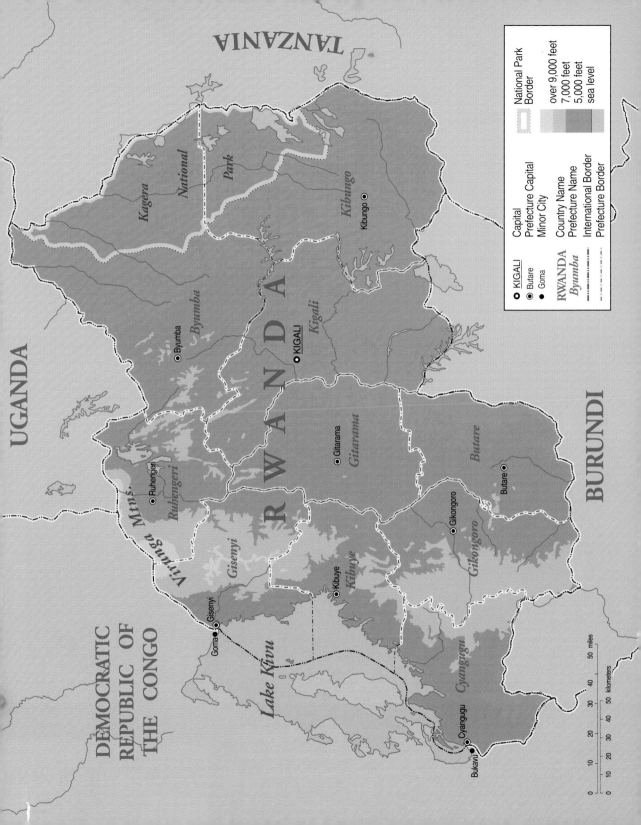

Since 1990 Rwanda has been plagued by a violent ethnic conflict between the Hutus and the Tutsis, the nation's two major **ethnic groups.** The height of this conflict came in 1994, when fighting erupted after a brief peace. The conflict has claimed the lives of nearly one million Rwandans and has created a massive refugee problem. Those involved in the fighting have included politicians, military staff, and ordinary citizens.

ETHNIC GROUPS

Rwanda's population is divided into three main ethnic groups. The country's earliest inhabitants, the Twa (also known as the Batwa), make up only about 1 percent of the population. The two largest ethnic groups in Rwanda are the Hutus (or Bahutu)—who before the civil war accounted for roughly 85 percent of the population—and the Tutsis (or Batutsi), who comprised about 14 percent of the population prior to the war. This ratio of Hutus to Tutsis has remained roughly the same for most of Rwanda's history. Hutus and Tutsis also dominate neighboring Burundi, in much the same ratio as they do in Rwanda. In addition, smaller numbers of Hutus and Tutsis live in Uganda, Tanzania, and the Democratic Republic of the Congo.

The Hutus and the Tutsis, along with the Twa, have lived together in Rwanda for nearly 1,000 years. Hutus and Tutsis share common social and cultural values. Both groups, as well as the Twa, speak Kinyarwanda, a Bantu language. Hutus and Tutsis live side by side in both the countryside and in urban areas, and there has been a great deal of intermarriage between the two groups. In addition, both groups prac-

Trygve Bølstad/Panos Pictures

Sometimes called the "Switzerland of Africa," Rwanda is covered with hills. The high altitude helps keep the tropical climate relatively cool.

Kigali, Rwanda's capital and its largest population center, is one of the few urban areas in the country. Nearly 95 percent of the Rwandan population lives in the countryside.

tice the Catholic and Protestant versions of the Christian faith. Throughout Rwanda's history, however, the ethnic labels have been synonymous with social division, and in the twentieth century this division has led to discrimination, violence, and political upheaval.

LAND AND POPULATION PRESSURE

Rwanda is a crowded country, and more than 95 percent of the population is rural. The best farming regions are the most densely populated, with sometimes as many as 1,100 people per square mile. The Butare and Ruhengeri prefectures, as well as the central uplands—where the altitude averages 5,000 to 7,000 feet above sea level—are some of the most fertile and populated regions in the country. In rural Rwanda, most people live on hills occupied by a number of families. Since agriculture is the main source of food and jobs for most Rwandans, farmland is a valuable commodity.

Rwandans use some of their farmland to raise livestock, especially cattle. Cows, in fact, are one of the most important possessions in Rwandan society. Some cattle are used for their milk or meat. Others are very thin and are not a source of food or drink. Instead they serve to represent a person's wealth and social standing in society.

The rest of the land is used to grow subsistence crops—such as peas, bananas, sweet potatoes, corn, beans, and peanuts. These crops help feed Rwanda's expanding population. In addition, Rwandans harvest cash crops, which are items that can be sold to people in Rwanda or in other nations in exchange for food or money. Coffee beans, for instance, are Rwanda's largest export

Lush, green gardens (left) *sprout from Rwandan farmland, which is among the most highly cultivated in the world. Bananas* (above) *are one of Rwanda's most significant subsistence crops.*

item and its biggest earner of foreign income. Rwandans also grow tea, cotton, and pyrethrum, a flower that's used to produce insecticides. Rwanda exports these items to European countries or to other African nations.

Competition for the best quality and the largest quantities of land in Rwanda has fueled social and ethnic ten-sions. Land has switched hands between the Hutus and the Tutsis many times over the past few centuries. The division of land has typ-ically coincided with political and economic power.

Adding to the population pressure is the country's birthrate—3.7 percent—one of the world's highest. The high birthrate causes the Rwandan population to in-crease by about 2.1 percent each year, which equates to adding about 168,000 people annually. Such a high number of citizens in a small area puts a lot of pressure on the land. Because the land must sus-tain so many people, it is sub-ject to intense farming. This leads to a high level of soil damage and contributes to the constant threat of famine in Rwanda. In 1990 more than 300 people died of starvation in southern Rwanda. One of the country's worst famines, in the 1920s, killed 50,000 Rwandans in one year.

Famine and malnutrition are also caused by the lack of arable land. Only about 35 percent of Rwanda's land can be used for farming, while 20 percent is pasture and 11 percent is forest. The remaining 34 percent of Rwanda contains marshes, swampland, protected national parks, volcanoes, wetlands, and woodland areas, as well as urban and mountainous regions. Farming is difficult, if not impossible, in all these areas.

The varying climate can be a challenge for farmers as well. Located just two degrees south of the equator, Rwanda is in a tropical region. But because of its high altitude, the country remains relatively cool, with an average daily temperature of about 68 degrees. Rwanda has four distinct seasons, two rainy and two dry, that can adversely affect farming, transportation, commerce, and communication. Periods of long rains, which can last for many days, typically occur from mid-March to mid-May. Shorter rains, often lasting only hours, take place from mid-October to mid-December. The short dry season runs from approximately mid-December through mid-March, whereas the long dry season usually occurs between mid-May and mid-October. The varied climate affects Rwandans' ability to produce enough food to survive.

Agriculture's importance to Rwanda is heightened by the fact that the country does not have many valuable minerals or manufactured products. It has a few natural resources, such as tin, clay, lime, gravel, and tungsten, but these are only useful within Rwanda. The country's main industries produce food and textiles. Small-scale industries within Rwanda also make paper, chemicals,

Rwanda's high birthrate is one of the reasons why the country is so crowded. Forty-seven percent of the Rwandan population is under the age of 15.

and rubber. Overall, industry and commerce employ only about 2 percent of Rwanda's population.

Until 1990 tourism was Rwanda's second largest foreign income source, earning between $8 million and $10 million a year for the country. Many tourists visited Rwanda to see its nearly extinct population of mountain gorillas. Half of the world's remaining mountain gorillas live in the Virunga Mountains, located in the northwestern part of the country, along the border with Uganda and the Democratic Republic of the Congo. In the past, Rwanda has also been a popular vacation destination for wealthy foreigners and European diplomats. Gisenyi, which lies on the shores of Lake Kivu, was a popular vacation spot, with its white sandy beaches, stucco hotels, outdoor cafés, and easy access from the Kigali airport. The recent conflict, however, has destroyed the tourism industry in Rwanda.

TRANSPORTATION AND COMMUNICATION

Although Rwanda has an extensive roadway system, there are only about 620 miles of paved roads, such as the one from Kigali to Gisenyi. The remaining 6,835 miles of roads are unpaved. Many rough, chewed-up dirt roads connect towns, but vehicles sometimes have difficulty traveling on them. During the rainy seasons, for instance, small landslides wash away or block many of these dirt roads. Few bridges exist, so certain areas are only navigable during the dry months. Since only a small percentage of Rwandans own cars and the country has no railway system, most Rwandans travel by bus or on foot and typically remain close to home. Rural Rwandans don't necessarily travel to towns or markets. Instead they tend to be very self-sufficient. Families usually live on clusters of land next to or near one another, so that if the crops in one field fail, another parcel of land may yield food to sustain several families.

Few Rwandans have telephones, which are too expensive to own and operate. Therefore, Rwandans exchange information mainly by word of mouth. There are several low-circulating newspapers that are either owned by the government or run by political parties and the Catholic Church, but these newspapers typically reach an elite audience. People in rural areas generally don't have access to the newspapers that are in print. Most Rwandans are avid radio listeners, making radio broadcasts the most effective way of reaching many people at once. The government-owned and operated radio station, called Radio Rwanda, reaches a wide number of people and is considered the main source of information for Rwandans.

The lack of access to independent media sources results in an easily manipulated public. The Rwandan media has fueled the ethnic conflict by spreading **propaganda** and rumors that create a climate of fear. Because rural Rwandan communities are relatively isolated and cannot obtain unbiased news and information, many Rwandans act on misinformation.

ETHNIC STRIFE

Ethnic conflicts can be caused by one issue or by a combination of factors. For instance, different religious, social, or political beliefs can

The Rwandan countryside is dotted with small, single-family farms. Most rural families rarely venture far from their ingo, a Kinyarwanda word for family enclosure or compound. As a result, there is little sense of unity among rural communities.

divide people. Discrimination against people based on their ethnic identity, social status, ancestry, wealth, education level, or the language they speak can also lead to conflict. In Rwanda's case, the Hutus and the Tutsis share a common language and a set of social values and have the same or similar religious beliefs. The clash between the two groups has resulted from social and political power struggles.

The Hutus and the Tutsis have a complex history. By the early 1800s, the Tutsis were politically powerful and held much of the best land in Rwanda. Meanwhile, the Hutus were mainly peasants, farmers, and unskilled laborers who had little political or social power. As a result, the Hutu and Tutsi peoples were divided along class lines. However, the political system was complex, and some Hutus held positions of power. In addition, intermarriage between the Hutus and the Tutsis was common, and identities were flexible. Hutu families that acquired wealth would come to be regarded as Tutsi. Conflicts, when they occurred, cut across ethnic lines, uniting one faction of Tutsis and Hutus against another.

When Rwanda became a German colony in the late nineteenth century, the social divisions became entrenched. From the late nineteenth to the mid-twentieth century, German and then Belgian colonial governments favored the Tutsis and exaggerated the existing class differences. This favoritism allowed Tutsis to gain greater control over Rwandan society. Tutsis acquired land and received positions in government and business. With the help of the colonial powers, the Tutsis were able to crush any Hutu resistance to Tutsi dominance. During this time, Hutus became second-class

citizens with little access to education and few means of improving their lives.

A change in attitude by the Belgian colonial authorities enabled many Hutus to gain access to education in the 1950s. This change not only allowed Hutus to move upward in social class but also gave them an increased awareness of their rights as Rwandan citizens. From then on, fuel for the Hutu-Tutsi conflict came partly from the discrimination many Hutus felt they had suffered under centuries of Tutsi rule and European colonization. An outgrowth of these feelings was the 1959 revolution, which led to social and political advancement for the Hutus. After 1959 ethnic discrimination was reversed and turned against the Tutsis. Hutu leaders insisted that, as the majority, the Hutu people should rule the country. Hutus came to dominate economic and political life—a situation that remained in place until the recent conflict.

The definitions of what it means to be a Hutu or a Tutsi have varied over the centuries. In early Rwandan society, occupation distinguished the Hutus from the Tutsis. Tutsis were cattle herders and Hutus were farmers. During the centuries of Tutsi rule in Rwanda, the Hutu and Tutsi labels became affiliated with social status—with Tutsis often having a higher social rank than Hutus had. Under colonialism, ethnic identity became associated with a combination of physical and social characteristics. European stereotypes defined Tutsis as the elite, tall, thin, and well-educated rulers and classified the Hutus as the short, stocky, uneducated peasants who comprised the general population. Although these stereotypes were not accurate, the ethnic labels and their corresponding physical and social characteristics stuck. Many Rwandans came to believe the stereotypes, even though intermarriage between the two groups was common.

By the mid- to late twentieth century, social status and appearance no longer defined ethnicity. Intermarriages between members of the two groups have made it virtually impossible to determine ethnic affiliation through physical features. In addition, Hutus and Tutsis no longer conform to the social stereotypes that were created by the European colonizers. Despite these changes, political **extremists** in Rwanda have continued to exploit ethnic differences, stereotypes, and past grievances to promote violence and to further their own agenda.

WHO'S FIGHTING WHOM?

In 1990 Rwanda's ethnic problems grew into a civil war. The main participants were the mostly Hutu Rwandan Armed Forces (FAR, in its French acronym) and a force of Tutsi exiles from Uganda known as the Rwandan Patriotic Front (RPF). This conflict raged until 1993, when the two sides agreed to a peace treaty. But in April 1994, after eight months of peace, the Rwandan civil war took a violent turn, grabbing the world's attention.

The 14 weeks of fighting that followed claimed the lives of more than 500,000 Rwandans. The conflict also forced many Rwandans to flee their homes and to settle in areas where they hoped they would be safe. These people ended up either in refugee camps located outside Rwanda or in displaced persons camps within the country. In these temporary settlements, the fleeing Rwandans built tentlike homes and received donations of food, water, medicine, and other supplies. Lack of food, medicine, and good sanitary conditions in many of these camps, however, caused deaths for several months after the war ended. And, although the civil war officially ended in 1994, the conflict continues to this day.

The origins of the conflict between Hutus and Tutsis go deep into Rwandan history, but the main cause of the civil war that started in 1990 was the issue of Tutsi exiles. Between 1959 and 1973, thousands of Tutsis were driven from Rwanda by the Hutu-led government. These expatriates, known as **Banyarwanda** (meaning "the people of Rwanda" in Kinyarwanda), had been living in neighboring countries, such as Uganda, Burundi, and Tanzania. During the 1980s, a group of Tutsi exiles in Uganda formed the RPF with the purpose of invading Rwanda. The main goals of the invasion were to enable the Tutsi exiles to return to Rwanda,

to end discrimination against the Tutsis, and to force the Rwandan government to make democratic reforms that would enable members of both ethnic groups to govern the country.

Rwandan president Juvenal Habyarimana and his party, the National Revolutionary Movement for Development (MRND, in its French acronym), were opposed to the return of the Tutsi exiles and wanted to maintain Hutu dominance. Prior to the 1993 peace treaty, Hutu extremists within the government, the MRND, and other political parties formed **militia groups** to instigate violence against Tutsi civilians and moderate Hutus who opposed the government. These militias, known as the Interahamwe (meaning "those who stand together" in Kinyarwanda), played a major role in the fighting that broke out in April 1994.

Political and military leaders, members of the extremist groups, and civilians in Rwanda have different views about running the country. Hutu extremists want to eliminate all Tutsis from Rwandan society and maintain control of the land

and government. Moderate Hutus, who are less radical than the extremists, want to share control of the country with the Tutsis. Similarly, many Tutsis are in favor of a multiparty government that would enable Tutsis and Hutus to hold offices and to run the country together. Some Tutsis, on the other hand, believe that the Tutsis should be the sole rulers of the country. Generally, average Hutus and Tutsis believe that after 1,000 years of living together in Rwanda, both groups must continue to share the land.

Some Rwandans claim no allegiance to any military or political group. They believe that the country's conflict is due to political rather than ethnic differences and make no ethnic distinction between their fellow citizens. When the war began, for instance, some Hutu and Tutsi civilians disregarded the extremist propaganda and helped save one another from the fighting. On the other hand, many civilians killed friends and neighbors solely because of their ethnic identity. ⊕

Juvenal Habyarimana

Belgium

Paul Kagame

MAJOR PLAYERS IN THE CONFLICT

Belgium Governed the territory of Ruanda-Urundi from 1919 to 1962. The Belgian administration was responsible for supporting Tutsi supremacy and creating an ethnic divide between Hutus and Tutsis. In the late 1950s, the Belgians began supporting Rwanda's Hutu majority, enabling the Hutus to gain control of the government and assert independence.

Habyarimana, Juvenal The president of Rwanda from 1973 to 1994. Originally an officer in the Rwandan army, Habyarimana overthrew the government of Grégoire Kayibanda in 1973 and instituted single-party rule.

Interahamwe Meaning "those who stand together" in Kinyarwanda. A civilian militia group organized by MRND party members that instigated violence against Tutsis and political opponents.

Kagame, Paul Leader of the Rwandan Patriotic Front (RPF) who became vice president and defense minister of Rwanda in 1994. He is believed to be the real head of the Rwandan government.

Kayibanda, Grégoire The first president of Rwanda. In the late 1950s, Kayibanda became an outspoken opponent of Tutsi dominance and a leader of the Hutu majority. As president, Kayibanda reversed decades of discrimination against the Hutus and oppressed the Tutsi minority.

National Revolutionary Movement for Development (MRND) The political party created and led by former president Juvenal Habyarimana. During most of Habyarimana's reign, all national and local government figures were MRND members. Hutu extremists within the MRND played a large role in organizing the violence of 1994.

Interahamwe

Rwandan Armed Forces (FAR) The Rwandan army. From 1990 to 1993, the mostly Hutu FAR defended Rwanda against the RPF invasion. After the resumption of the civil war in 1994, FAR soldiers took part in the massacres of Tutsis and moderate Hutus.

Rwandan Patriotic Front (RPF) A political and military organization created and led by Tutsi exiles in Uganda. Fred Rwigema and Paul Kagame, two Tutsi officers in Uganda's National Resistance Army, established the RPF in the late 1980s.

Rwandan Patriotic Front

United Nations (UN) A nongovernmental agency set up in 1945 to work for world peace. In 1946 the UN granted Ruanda-Urundi to Belgium as a trust territory. In 1993 the UN created a special force, the United Nations Assistance Mission to Rwanda (UNAMIR), to oversee the installation of a transitional government in Rwanda.

United Nations

1

THE RECENT CONFLICT AND ITS EFFECTS

Dead and decaying bodies were piled high along the roadsides in Goma, Zaire—a town on Rwanda's northwestern border—awaiting trucks to deliver them to mass graves. Swarming down the center of the streets were thousands of hungry and exhausted Rwandans. These survivors of disease and war—most of them Hutus—had walked up to 150 miles fleeing Tutsi forces fighting for control of Rwanda. The Tutsi army, known as the RPF, was sweeping across Rwanda in search of those responsible for killings that had begun in April 1994 and that had left at least 500,000 Rwandan Tutsis and moderate Hutus dead.

The fleeing Rwandans included people of all ages and occupations. Some were dressed in expensive suits and skirts. Others wore tat-

The 14 weeks of warfare and bloodshed during the Rwandan civil war created one of the largest refugee movements the world had ever witnessed.

United Nations Commission for Refugees

tered clothes that were ripped and soiled from working in the fields. Many walked barefoot, their feet swollen and aching from the trek. Some of the people had nothing with them except

the clothes on their backs. Others were carrying their few belongings. Often people grew tired of carrying their belongings and discarded them along the roadsides. Sometimes they let go of their children, too.

Meanwhile, at an orphanage located in central Rwanda, about 250 children—mostly Tutsis—finished their evening meals of thick, green porridge. After dinner and cleanup, a volunteer doctor examined the children, some of whom were suffering from such deadly diseases as AIDS, tuberculosis, and malaria. This was the typical routine at the orphanage, one of about 100 orphanages in Rwanda and in neighboring countries. These orphanages, as well as refugee camps in and around Rwanda, collectively were home to about one million children at the height of Rwanda's civil war crisis. Many had escaped Rwanda with relatives, but hundreds of thousands were orphaned or separated from their parents during the war. Some children saw their parents killed, whereas others were abandoned by parents who could no longer feed or care for them.

PEACE BREAKS DOWN

Since 1990 the RPF had been fighting the government of President Juvenal Habyarimana. For nearly 20 years, the Habyarimana regime had ruled Rwanda as a single-party dictatorship. This government discriminated against Tutsis and those Hutus who did not come from the president's home region and blocked the return of Tutsi exiles from Burundi, Uganda, and Tanzania. The RPF offensive of 1990 not only aimed to return the exiles but also to create a multiparty government that would give equal treatment to members of both ethnic groups.

After three years of low-level fighting, which tended to occur in isolated regions, members of the RPF and President Habyarimana's government signed a peace ac-cord called the Arusha Peace Agreement. This treaty, which went into effect August 4, 1993, laid out a plan to allow all Tutsi exiles to return home and to merge the mostly Tutsi RPF forces and the mostly Hutu Rwandan Armed Forces (FAR) into one army. In addition, the agreement created a plan that would lead to multiparty elections in 1995. In other words, the Rwandan people would elect a government consisting of Hutus and Tutsis.

Some Rwandans—particularly the Hutu extremists within the Habyarimana government and the ruling MRND party—were not happy with the peace plan. The Hutu extremists were completely opposed to sharing power with Rwanda's Tutsi and other, more moderate political groups. But many Rwandans from both ethnic groups hoped that the peace treaty would end the Hutu-Tutsi conflict. Under the accord's terms, Faustin Twagiramungu, a moderate Hutu politician, was named prime minister. He was expected to lead a transitional government for 18 months, at which point multiparty elections would take place.

With the signing of the Arusha Peace Agreement, it looked as if Rwanda might be on the verge of solving its ethnic problems. But in April 1994, the unexpected death of President Habyarimana in a mysterious plane crash rekindled the civil war. This renewed violence was wide-spread. Large numbers of civilians, militia groups, and military forces were involved in the fighting.

VIOLENCE AND RETALIATION

After the death of the president, Hutu extremists took over the government. They immediately accused the RPF of causing the plane crash and used the death of the president as an excuse to renew the civil war and incite violence against Tutsis and political opponents. Soon after the crash, the extremist Interahamwe militias organized and spearheaded a campaign of violence against Tutsis and moderate Hutus who had supported the Arusha accords. Over the course of 14 weeks, these militias—along with FAR members, civil authorities, and Hutu civilians—killed at least 500,000 Tutsis and Hutu moderates.

The widespread killing targeted men, women, and children, many of whom sought refuge from their attackers inside churches, stadiums, schools, and universities. In some cases, the Hutu militias intentionally herded people into these places to kill them. In Kibuye, for example, a group of Hutu soldiers and militia members told thousands of Tutsis they would be safe inside the town's soccer stadium. When the stadium was full, they gunned down the 7,000 Tutsis inside. Those who were wounded during the shooting were then killed with machetes and knives. In a church about 25 miles east of Kigali, Hutu militias massacred 1,200 Tutsis—half of them children—with semi-automatic weapons, knives, bats, and spears. Many Tutsis built secret hiding places in or near their homes and stayed there for months, often without much food or water.

Across the country, Hutu extremists used propaganda to urge Hutus to kill their Tutsi neighbors and anyone suspected of being an RPF supporter. Government and extremist radio stations warned that the RPF wanted to reestablish Tutsi dominance. Hutu militias often directed and sometimes forced commune leaders and civil authorities to organize the slaughter of Tutsis in their area. Because bullets were expensive, militia members used machetes, knives, and clubs to kill people. Sometimes, those about to be killed had an option— they could pay for bullets and be shot or else they would be slaughtered with machetes and handmade weapons. Hutu soldiers and militia members also raped thousands of Tutsi women.

AP/Wide World Photos

The death of President Habyarimana (below left) provided the spark for weeks of anti-Tutsi violence (facing page). Throughout the country, Tutsis were attacked by Interahamwe members, soldiers, and sometimes even neighbors.

At the time of the conflict, all Rwandans were required to carry a national identification card that indicated whether they were Hutu or Tutsi. At roadblocks around the country, militia members would check the identity cards of those trying to flee the fighting. Citizens whose cards listed them as Tutsi were pulled from cars and killed.

Militia members and civil authorities coerced and, in many cases, threatened civilians to get them to take part in the killing. As a result, some Hutus killed Tutsis who

Reuters/Corinne Dufka/Archive Photos

According to the Rwandan government, nearly one million Rwandans—including the more than 500,000 Tutsis and Hutu moderates killed by Hutu militias—lost their lives during the 14 weeks of fighting. But unofficial estimates by several aid organizations claim the death toll could be as high as 2.7 million. There is no way of knowing how many people were actually killed. The fighting occurred quickly, and aid workers often buried the victims in mass graves without counting them. In some cases, killers disposed of bodies quickly to mask the numbers of people killed.

In addition, the RPF offensive forced an estimated 2.3 million Rwandans, mainly Hutus, to flee to Zaire, Burundi, and Tanzania. About 2.1 million other Hutus resettled in regions within Rwanda where they hoped they would be safe. Since the RPF attacked from the north and marched through Rwanda to the southwest, the majority of fleeing refugees ended up in Burundi, in Zaire, or in southern and western Rwanda.

had been longtime friends or neighbors. But in other instances, Hutus risked their lives to save Tutsis, hiding them in their homes despite the risk of death. Some Rwandans believed that the Hutu-Tutsi conflict was a political problem, rather than the result of ethnic hatred. The main concern for these people was to take care of their land and families. In the climate of fear and hysteria, however, many succumbed to the violence.

Soon after the attacks against Tutsis and moderate Hutus began, the RPF retaliated, attacking from the north. RPF soldiers chased the Hutu militias and FAR soldiers into southern and western Rwanda, fighting them with AK-47s and small artillery. Within weeks, RPF soldiers had fought their way southward from Uganda and from bases within Rwanda to overtake Kigali. By July 1994, the RPF was in control of most of Rwanda. By mid-July a cease-fire was in effect. But although the RPF had ended the violence, Hutu civilians who feared reprisals left the country in droves.

Zaire received the largest group of refugees. About one million Rwandans arrived in the country during the summer of 1994. At one point, about 10,000 refugees were crossing into Goma, Zaire, per hour. The town of Bukavu, located on Lake Kivu in southern Zaire, received 360,000 refugees. When Zairian officials closed the border at Bukavu one day, refugees who were desperate to leave Rwanda even jumped into the lake and swam across to Zaire, while others made the crossing in canoes. In the meantime, about 180,000 Rwandans escaped to Burundi, and 600,000 refugees fled to Tanzania. In fact, nearly 250,000 refugees fled to Ngara, Tanzania, a small town on the border of Rwanda, within a 24-hour period in April. This was the fastest exodus of so many people ever to be recorded in the world. Several months later, Zaire received about 800,000 refugees in just a few days. This huge movement of people became a humanitarian crisis.

In the refugee camps, people did whatever they could to survive. In addition to con-

At this refugee camp run by the United Nations High Commissioner for Refugees (UNHCR), aid workers provided refugees with plastic sheeting to create shelters (right). *Despite the situation, many refugees tried to create some semblance of ordinary life* (below).

United Nations Commission for Refugees

structing homes, many refugees built restaurants, churches, and small stores, where they sold everything from tree branches and cigarettes to matches and soda. Some people grew corn on patches of land no bigger than a couch, while others collected wood, bamboo, and other items to sell. Illegal businesses also thrived in the refugee camps. Refugees in Bukavu, Zaire, often traveled to Cyangugu in southwestern Rwanda to loot the streets, shops, and homes there. After gathering tires, car seats, engine parts, toilets, and doors, they would sell these

stolen items in the camp. People used the money from these illegal businesses to buy food and other items to help them survive. As refugees went about their daily duties and tried to survive, aid workers from **nongovernmental organizations** (NGOs) built pit-style latrines, buried bodies, and provided clothing, food, water, and medical treatment.

Starvation, dehydration, exhaustion, and diseases such as cholera and dysentery had a devastating effect on the camps, killing tens of thousands of refugees. To bury people quickly and to pre-

TENSION REMAINS

The events of 1994 devastated Rwanda. International observers estimated that the war and the ensuing refugee crisis left only five million people in Rwanda. In addition, the conflict destroyed the country's infrastructure and left its economy in ruins.

Rwanda had long been one of the world's poorest nations, but by 1997 it was considered the second least developed country in the world. With certain areas completely abandoned, roads and fields had become overgrown, requiring significant work to make them usable again. As people resettled, they were often faced with the challenge of tilling wild fields and having to wait several seasons to harvest crops. In some regions, this caused food shortages and famines.

Civilians, especially children, suffered significantly. Many were caught in the middle of fighting and killed. Others were severely traumatized by what they had witnessed around them, such as the murders of friends and family members. Those children who escaped have had to learn how to live with

vent the spread of disease, NGO workers stacked uncovered bodies in mass graves. Once the number dropped to less than 200 deaths per day, the bodies were wrapped in reed mats and covered with a mixture of dirt and lime. A mass grave bigger than a football field in the middle of the Mugunga camp was one burial site for the victims of disease. A lone white cross next to the grave was a constant reminder to refugees and NGO workers of the disaster that had struck the region.

these memories. They also have had to learn how to take care of themselves. One aid organization reported that by 1998 about 300,000 Rwandan children who had been orphaned or abandoned by their parents during the war were still looking after themselves and had no adult supervision.

Since the end of the war, Rwanda has been trying to

Epidemics

Clean drinking water was very hard and, at times, impossible to obtain during the height of the Rwandan refugee crisis. Most of the refugees in Zaire had settled in a park near Lake Kivu. The lake, however, was poisoned with methane gas, which had killed all the wildlife in the area. The gas had been created by rotting organic material at the lake's bottom. Lake Kivu was also contaminated with dead bodies and human excrement, creating harmful bacteria. The organizations running the camps could not provide enough clean water for everyone. Out of desperation, many refugees continued drinking water from the lake.

The lack of clean drinking water in the refugee camps resulted in major outbreaks of cholera and dysentery. Cholera, a bacterial disease, can cause severe dehydration and, if not treated, death. Cholera is treated with a simple solution of water and salt. Dysentery, an intestinal disease, results in severe diarrhea and requires an expensive five-day treatment of antibiotics. Because the camps could not adequately treat either of these diseases, thousands of refugees died. During the long rainy season, diseases spread even faster among people in the crowded refugee camps, causing many more deaths. Outbreaks of cholera and dysentery caused a catastrophe in Goma, killing almost 2,000 people a day. Overall, disease killed about 50,000 refugees in 1994.

© Charles Caratini/Sygma

A mass grave at the Goma refugee camp

get back on its feet. After the war ended, the Rwandan government urged refugees to return to the country. Small-scale voluntary repatriation began in August, and by late 1994, buses were running between Goma and Kigali to transport refugees back home. By the fall of 1995, 300,000 people had repatriated, but the process was slow. Then, in late 1996, there was a massive return of refugees from Zaire and Tanzania.

The Rwandan government hoped that the return of the refugees would close down the camps, which had become a haven for the remnants of the Hutu militias. Since the end of the civil war, militia members had been using the camps to regroup and plan new attacks against the Rwandan government. The government believed that closing the camps would put an end to the attacks.

The Rwandan government has welcomed the return of the refugees, but there has been violence during the repatriation process. Some Rwandans believe that the returning Hutus fled because they were guilty of taking part in the massacres of Tutsis and moderate Hutus. Villagers have attacked returning Hutus because of these beliefs, whether they are true or not. Adding to Rwanda's problems is the influx of Tutsi exiles from Uganda and Burundi, who returned to Rwanda after the RPF victory. These people have taken over abandoned homes, businesses, and land and are unwilling to return them to their original owners. Many refugees who have returned to Rwanda are too afraid to go home because they fear that they will be attacked if they try to reclaim their property. Many people remain displaced within Rwanda.

Another contentious issue in Rwanda is justice. The Rwandan government wants those responsible for the violence punished and has arrested thousands of Hutus in pursuit of that goal. As of 1998, the government had arrested nearly 120,000 people for taking part in the violence against Tutsis and Hutu moderates in 1994. Many of those arrested have not been officially charged with a crime, while others have waited years for a trial. In addition, the high number of arrests has created another problem—overcrowded jails where prisoners live in unsanitary and unhealthy conditions. Human rights groups are concerned about the situation.

The civil war is officially over, but fighting continues between the forces of the new Rwandan government and what is left of the Hutu militias. Raids, uprisings, and ambushes have been instigated by members of the ousted government, soldiers, and civilians who are either seeking revenge or trying to reclaim their property. This continuing violence threatens to destroy any hopes of reconciliation between Hutus and Tutsis.

As the history of Rwanda will show, Hutus and Tutsis have more than recent events to overcome. The two groups have lived side by side for centuries, yet issues of status and ethnicity have clouded their relationship and have led to discrimination and violence throughout the twentieth century. To better understand the roots of the violence, it is necessary to explore Rwanda's beginnings and uncover the myths and misinterpretations that have shaped its history. ⊕

CHAPTER

2

THE CONFLICT'S ROOTS

Little is known about the origins of the groups that populate modern-day Rwanda. For thousands of years, various African peoples migrated in and out of the region. But by the fifteenth century, the descendants of modern-day Rwandans were established in the region.

The Twa people were hunter-gatherers who lived off the animals and plants of the densely forested region. The Hutus based their livelihood on agriculture. Hutu families lived on and cultivated certain areas of land but were less interested in selling their crops than in producing enough food to feed their families. The Tutsis were nomadic cattle herders who didn't live in permanent settlements but rather stayed in one area temporarily. When pasture in that area had been used up, they moved in search of new

territory. This nomadic lifestyle forced Tutsi men to become skilled warriors, because they had to be able to fight people to protect their cattle and families when they entered new territory.

The primary social unit in this society was the hill on which a family lived. To ensure survival, each Hutu household belonged to an extended family group, called a clan, that worked together to grow crops. In some cases, clans banded together with other clans to form a kingdom, which was ruled by a king called the *bahinza*. Many of these farming kingdoms were spread across the countryside. Instead of having one ruler for the entire Rwandan territory, there were many kings, each of whom was in charge of a particular clan. Like the Hutus, the Tutsis were also organized by clan. In some cases,

clans included both Hutus and Tutsis.

Although the origins of the Hutu and Tutsi labels are not known, most modern-day scholars agree that they were not ethnic distinctions. Rather they signified occupational categories that distinguished those who were predominantly farmers from those who were mainly cattle herders. In addition, the labels indicated a difference in status.

In many African societies, the ownership of cattle represents wealth and social status. Good fighting abilities have also traditionally signified power, prestige, and strength. Because Tutsi men were skilled warriors and had an abundance of cattle, they believed they were superior to the Hutus, who owned fewer cattle and had inferior fighting abilities. Both groups looked down on the Twa, who made up a small per-

Before the arrival of widespread agricultural practices, Rwanda was heavily forested. While the Hutus in ancient Rwanda concentrated primarily on farming (left), the Tutsis focused on cattle herding (above).

centage of the population and neither farmed the land nor owned cattle.

TUTSI DOMINANCE

Although Tutsis were greatly outnumbered by Hutus, they used their physical strength and mobility to gain control of what would become Rwanda without large-scale fighting. The beginning of Tutsi dominance started with a single Tutsi clan, the Nyiginya, which owned a large number of cattle and wanted to expand its cattle-grazing territory. This clan first achieved political dominance in central Rwanda and over time expanded by incorporating other clans and taking land from the Hutus.

By the 1500s, the Nyiginya clan had established a small monarchy—the kingdom of Rwanda, based on a small area of modern-day Rwanda—under their king, called the *mwami*. The first king of this centralized monarchy was Mwami Mibambwe I Mutabazi. The mwami, who was considered a divine being, owned all the land within the kingdom and was in charge of land distribution. Typically, he awarded land to members of the

The Problem of History

It is often difficult to trace the history of a culture, especially if that culture does not have a written record of the past. For centuries the early history of Rwanda was recorded in oral traditions—such as songs, sayings, and stories—after the country had been settled by the Hutus and the Tutsis. Many of these oral records may be accurate, but there is no way of knowing for sure. When stories are passed down from generation to generation, they can be altered and changed. Sometimes this happens unintentionally, but other times these changes are meant to achieve personal or political benefits. In addition, not all aspects of society or all historic events are recorded over time. Instead only certain, selective events or beliefs survive for future generations to learn about.

The stories that can be traced back to a society's early history may not be representative of the beliefs of everyone in that society. And not all events have been recorded. Often those in power are in charge of which stories, ideas, and beliefs are recorded. In early Rwanda, court historians handed down stories selected by the Tutsi royalty. In some cases, these stories were biased or based on myths that had been created by the Tutsis to support their dominance. Therefore, many stories that were considered "official" Rwandan history asserted the notion that the Tutsis were supreme and that they had been chosen by the gods to rule.

One ancient Rwandan myth tells the story of Gihanga, the first Rwandan, who fell from heaven with three sons—Gahutu, Gatwa, and Gatutsi. According to the story, Gihanga was to choose which son would succeed him. To find out who was most worthy, he tested them. Each son was given a pot of milk to watch over during the night. When the morning came, Gihanga found that Gatwa had drunk his milk, while Gahutu had fallen asleep and knocked over his pot. Gatutsi, however, had watched over his pot the whole night. For Gihanga this meant that Gatutsi was the most responsible and thus was meant to succeed Gihanga. As a result, Gahutu was ordered to serve Gatutsi.

Nyiginya lineage and to the more powerful Tutsi elite. In this centralized monarchy, most Tutsis were cattle herders, soldiers, and administrators, whereas most Hutus were farmers. The Tutsi elite created a number of myths and legends to justify the king's status and Tutsi superiority.

The foundation of this hierarchy was a **feudal system**—called *ubuhake* in the southern and central regions of the kingdom and *ubukonde* in the north—that offered incentives to both the Hutu farmers and the landholding Tutsis. The ubuhake was an oral agreement between a client (peasant) and a patron (lord), through which the client provided crops and performed services for the lord. In return, the lord gave the client cattle, offered protection from threatening forces, and allowed the client to use his land. Most of the lords were Tutsis, and most of the clients were Hutus. Although the ubuhake had benefits for both groups, it still established a strong social, economic, and political divide between the Hutus and the Tutsis. The domination

© Africa-Museum Tervuren (Belgium)

In ancient Rwanda, the Hutu and Tutsi labels had less to do with ethnicity than with occupation and status. Despite their different roles in society, Tutsis (below) *and* Hutus (right) *spoke the same language and observed many of the same customs.*

Archive Photos

of the Hutus by the Tutsis was further reinforced through the development of an intricate hierarchy that enabled the mwami to successfully rule over his territory.

The mwami's territory was divided into districts run by chiefs. Collectively, the chiefs made up the Council of Great Chiefs and functioned as the mwami's advisers. The mwami's districts were organized into hills, called *umusozi*, run by hill chiefs. The hills were then split into neighborhoods, with each neighborhood having a subchief. The mwami also had administrative chiefs. An army chief was responsible for the protection of the region. The land chief collected a tribute—a tax paid to a lord or ruler in exchange for protec-

tion—from each inhabitant in the form of agricultural produce. A cattle chief collected a tribute in the form of livestock. Those in office, especially the mwami, benefited from these taxes. The mwami used some of the agricultural produce and livestock he collected to pay his chiefs and military officers. He did this to ensure their loyalty to him. More than 95 percent of these administrative posts were held by Tutsis. Under this stratified system, the monarchy and most military men, most chiefs, and most

> *Status, rather than ethnicity, defined a person's social ranking and privileges. As a result, some ethnic Hutus had Tutsi status and held positions of power within the Rwandan hierarchy.*

subchiefs were Tutsis, whereas only a few chiefs and soldiers were Hutus.

For centuries the Hutus and Tutsis lived under this hierarchy. Other than the difference in status, however, these groups were united by many common traits. They shared the same language—Kinyarwanda—the same social customs, and the same value systems. There were some differences in beliefs, but these distinctions typically existed between those of separate classes in society. The Hutus and the Tutsis also worshiped the same high god, called Lyngomde, and many of the same lesser deities, such as Lyengombe and Nyabingi. These similarities have led many modern scholars to believe that the Hutus and the Tutsis were essentially the same people and not distinct ethnic groups.

The Rwandan hierarchy was founded on wealth and status, not ethnicity. Because status was based on owner-ship of cattle, an elite group of cattle owners—who were by definition Tutsis—typically owned most of the land and held the higher positions in society. But the ubuhake system allowed for upward mobility, meaning that average Hutus could become Tutsis if they were to obtain a certain amount of cattle. In this way, a person could have Hutu ethnicity but have the social status of a Tutsi. Therefore, they would be considered a Tutsi. Similarly, poorer Tutsis were considered Hutus if they didn't own enough livestock. Status, rather than ethnicity, defined a person's social ranking and privileges. As a result, some ethnic Hutus had Tutsi status and held positions of power within the Rwandan hierarchy.

One of the biggest challenges for a the mwami was ensuring that all citizens were devoted to him. The feudal hierarchy did a good job of keeping control over people around the region, but the most devout followers lived near the mwami. Although the monarchy was strong, its reach did not extend to all areas of the kingdom. The farther away from the mwami's head-quarters, the less supportive people were of him. For instance, in the northwestern region of the kingdom, where many Hutus lived, the mwami had little support.

Even after the establishment of the Tutsi monarchy, independent Hutu principalities existed in the region, and they did not follow the orders of the mwami. Because the ubuhake system did not extend to these areas, the status distinction between the Hutus and the Tutsis was less clear. It wasn't until the nineteenth century that the Tutsi monarchy was able to extend its rule to these areas.

COLONIAL AUTHORITY

Beginning in the sixteenth century, European merchants began exploring commercial interests on the African continent. By the nineteenth century, some nations of Europe had decided to exert political control in Africa and to expand their colonial empires.

The Twa

The Twa *(below)* are an indigenous people, recognized as the first true inhabitants of Rwanda. As hunter-gatherers, the Twa lived off Rwanda's lush forests and abundant wildlife. But after the Hutus and the Tutsis had established themselves in Rwanda, the Twa's forest habitat began to shrink. Hutu farmers cut down trees to create farmland, while Tutsi cattle owners cleared forests to make pasture. Over the centuries, much of Rwanda's forests disappeared. Most Twa became tenants, paying for land with labor. Some, however, were still able to eke out a living in Rwanda's remaining woodlands. By the late twentieth century, government policies and the creation of protected wildlife areas forced most Twa to live on small plots of land that provided room for cultivation.

Throughout much of their history, the Twa have existed on the margins of Rwandan society. Physically short and greatly outnumbered by Hutus and Tutsis, they have been viewed by both groups as subhuman and uncivilized. This has led to much abuse and mistreatment at the hands of both Hutu and Tutsi. Although in precolonial Rwanda the Tutsi monarchy employed some Twa as soldiers and entertainers, Twa were not allowed to participate in the ubuhake system and to gain status. After the 1959 revolution, the government forcibly removed many Twa families from their land, and Hutu farmers regularly stole land from the Twa. During the violence of 1994, Hutu militias killed members of the Twa group for their past relationship with the Tutsi monarchy.

© Betty Press/Panos Pictures

European leaders and merchants believed that Africa could be an important outlet for exports, as well as a source of income. Before long Britain, France, Belgium, Italy, Portugal, Spain, and Germany all were scrambling to control territory across the continent.

Located in the heart of East Africa, the region that includes modern-day Rwanda and Burundi was one of the last areas on the African continent to attract European explorers. The area was landlocked, and the terrain was mountainous and lush. In addition, the region's ruling class—the Tutsis—were such good warriors that the Europeans found it difficult to enter the territory. During the 1800s, several British explorers traveled along the outskirts of what would become Rwanda, but it wasn't until 1894 that the first European—a German explorer named Count von Gotzen—made contact with the central areas of the region.

By the mid-1890s, Germany had obtained colonial rights to Rwanda. But the Belgians and the British were also interested in this territory because they both controlled nearby territories. Over the next few years, these three European nations went through numerous land disputes over the boundaries of each region they controlled in East Africa. As a result, it wasn't until 1910 that Germany, Belgium, and Britain finally agreed on the region's boundaries. The Germans became the official rulers of the region that included modern-day Rwanda and Burundi. Although two separate and distinct kingdoms existed in this area, Germany fused them into a single territory, which they called Ruanda-Urundi. (Although it was one territory, Germany governed Ruanda and Urundi under different policies.)

Colonialism had a strong impact on Rwanda and on the relationship between the Hutus and the Tutsis. In Rwanda the Germans observed the hierarchy that had been established by the Tutsi monarchy and decided that the Tutsis were superior to the Hutus. This belief was based not only on the difference in social status between the two groups, but also on racial theories that placed the Tutsis above the Hutus.

The German government named Dr. Richard Kandt, an

Dr. Richard Kandt was the first governor of Ruanda-Urundi. Germany's small administrative staff made it necessary to rule indirectly through the Tutsi monarchy.

explorer and scientist, to be the first governor of Ruanda-Urundi. The Germans ruled Rwanda indirectly through the Tutsi monarchy. Rather than change the entire governmental structure, which would have cost a great deal of money and required many administrators, the Germans kept the hierarchical system.

Dr. Kandt worked with the mwami and his chiefs to govern Rwanda. Because the Germans didn't station many of their people in the colony, they relied on the Tutsis to oversee the territory and to maintain the loyalty of the people.

The German military helped the Tutsis reinforce their rule by exerting power whenever necessary. For instance, in 1912 the Germans took action against rebellious Hutus in the northwest, where Tutsi authority had never been fully accepted. During the military maneuver, German soldiers burned Hutu homes, destroyed crops, and killed Hutu leaders. With German military support, the mwami was able to extend his territory and to strengthen Tutsi dominance in Rwanda. In addition, the Germans extended the ubuhake system to all areas of Rwanda. In return the Tutsi monarchy fully supported the German administration.

The Germans devised plans to improve the region's economy and infrastructure, but few significant projects were ever completed. German colonial rulers organized a simple judicial system and set up a small-scale communication network. But, with limited German staff stationed in the country, Rwanda experienced little growth economically, socially, or politically. The Germans did establish coffee plantations, which had not existed in the region before this time, and coffee beans became a cash crop that could be exported to other countries for money. By developing coffee as a cash crop, the Germans established a monetary economy in Ruanda. Until this stage, the Hutus and the Tutsis had exchanged goods, produce, cattle, and labor as payments.

In addition, the German administration forced Rwanda's citizens to pay a monetary tax to the German government. Musinga—Rwanda's mwami at the time—opposed this tax for fear that it might decrease his power. Some historians believe that as a result of the tax, Hutus began viewing the Germans as their leaders and protectors, as well as the stronger force in their society.

The Germans also brought in Catholic and Protestant missionaries, who encouraged Rwandans to adopt Christian beliefs and traditions. Some continued to follow their traditional beliefs, while others mixed the two. German priests established Christian mission schools to educate the Tutsi elite. Under this educational system, few Hutus gained access to secondary and higher education. The Tutsi elite took advantage of this educational system to further distance themselves from the Hutus.

BELGIAN RULE

When World War I (1914–1918) broke out, the Belgians, who were still interested in Ruanda-Urundi, fought the Germans for control of this region. Many Tutsis joined forces with the Belgians and fought against the Germans, who were outnumbered and overpowered. By 1916 Belgium had gained military control of the territory.

The Belgians initially wanted Ruanda-Urundi so they could exchange it for a territory belonging to Britain. But this attempt failed, and the League of Nations—a postwar organization of nations created to maintain world peace—gave Ruanda-Urundi to Belgium under a mandate (a formal order). The mandate dictated that Belgium had to maintain order in the territory and to create a more balanced government in which both Hutus and Tutsis were represented. The Belgians were further required to improve the territory's educational and health systems. By the mid-1920s, Belgium had officially accepted responsibility for Ruanda-Urundi.

The Belgians employed a governing strategy in Rwanda similar to that of the Germans, ruling through the Tutsi monarchy and using the hierarchical structure to enforce their policies. They found that this type of rule was very effective, because the population was scattered across the territory, making communication and transportation slow and difficult. The Belgians, like the Germans, also favored the Tutsi ethnic group and allowed them to retain strong political and social control over the territory. They believed that the Tutsis were better than the Hutus and should rule because of their

CHAPTER 2 *The Conflict's Roots*

Mwami Musinga discusses matters with a Belgian administrator. Although the Belgians reduced the powers of the mwami, their policies further reinforced the social and political dominance of the Tutsis.

"undeniable intellectual superiority" and "ruling potential." The Belgians allowed the Tutsi elite to remain in power while colonial officials tried to sort out some of the territory's social and economic problems.

The Belgians initially introduced reforms in the political system that enhanced their power in the region. While they believed that the Tutsis should be the ruling class, they wanted to introduce gradual social changes that would make Rwanda more efficient and productive. They altered the ubuhake system to stimulate economic growth and bridge the economic and social gap between the Hutus and Tutsis. They reduced from two days to one the number of days in a week a Hutu client had to perform work for a Tutsi patron. They also eliminated some of the mwami's power. Another major change was the elimination of all tributes, except those paid to the mwami. As a result, a patron could no longer demand a tribute from a client for protection. The Belgians hoped that these changes would encourage economic development in the colony.

At the same time, the Belgians reinforced Tutsi rule even more than the Germans had. They fused the land chief, cattle chief, and army chiefs into one position, thereby creating a more efficient and tightly organized bureaucracy. The Belgians then removed Hutu chiefs and subchiefs from power in the north and replaced them with Tutsis. They also encouraged the sons of Tutsi chiefs and subchiefs to enroll at mission schools so they could get the education needed to obtain civil service and government positions. Meanwhile, the Belgian administration continued to deny Hutus access to schooling. For example, in 1925 Rwanda's Nyanza École pour Fils des Chefs, a government

Racial Theories

The German and Belgian colonial administrators viewed Rwandan society through a lens of ethnic and racial stereotypes. Their views were based on nineteenth-century European racial theories, which promoted the idea that the Caucasoid (white) and Negroid (black) races had evolved separately and that the white race was inherently superior.

Noting the physical differences between Hutus and Tutsis, German colonists felt that the two groups must be from different racial stock. They argued that the Tutsis exhibited features that were closer to those of Europeans than they were to those of other Africans. Some anthropologists claimed that the Tutsis were Hamitic peoples—considered by European scientists to be the lowest branch of the Caucasoid race—who had come from the north to conquer and rule Rwanda. This conclusion led the Europeans to decide that the superior Tutsis were born to rule over the inferior Hutus and Twa. It has also led to the long-held belief that the Tutsis invaded Rwanda and conquered other groups. Modern-day historians have disproven this theory.

The theories of the European colonizers added a racial element to Rwandan society that had not previously existed. Over time the Tutsis and Hutus came to share these views. The Tutsis were especially receptive to these views, which bolstered their feelings of superiority. The feelings of inferiority among Hutus would turn into resentment and lead to anti-Tutsi violence. Hutu leaders would later cling to these racial theories, arguing that the Hutus were the country's only legitimate inhabitants and that the Tutsi "invaders" did not belong in Rwanda.

school in the town of Nyanza, had 349 students, all of whom were Tutsis. These policies reinforced the notion of Tutsi supremacy and Hutu subordination.

During its colonial occupation of Ruanda-Urundi, Belgium didn't develop the territory as much as other European countries had developed their African colonies. The Rwandan infrastructure did receive some attention, but no strong, local transportation system was established, nor did Belgium advance Rwandan industry or manufacturing. Instead, the Belgians chose to focus on exploiting the colony's natural resources, shipping tons of raw materials, such as tea, coffee, crops, and minerals, to Europe and the United States.

A major famine in 1928–1929 left about 50,000 Rwandans dead and forced Belgium to take action. Hoping to improve Rwanda's economic situation and to enable the colony to become more self-sufficient, the Belgians encouraged the development of more agricultural and cash crops. They hoped that the territory could produce an excess of food, so that if there was a poor harvest one year, Rwandans wouldn't have to rely on Belgium or other countries for food. Coffee production was increased so that Rwanda could make financial gains through coffee exports. But as a result of increased cultivation, the fertile land became severely overworked and agricultural production decreased.

CHAPTER 2 *The Conflict's Roots*

To meet their goal of making the colony self-sufficient, the Belgians established a new tax. It required each Hutu male to grow non-seasonal food crops on 20 acres of land, in addition to the land he cultivated for himself. The Belgians made the Tutsi chiefs enforce this policy among the peasants, establishing an oppressive, slave-like system. If a Hutu didn't produce the required amount of crops, the Belgians punished the Hutu's Tutsi chief. This system put pressure on the chiefs to make sure the Hutu peasants harvested plenty of crops. Therefore, the Tutsi chiefs often physically abused the Hutus to make them work. Many Tutsi chiefs took advantage of this situation as well, continuing to demand the traditional tribute payments from their clients. While the Hutu peasantry became increasingly impoverished, the Tutsi elite grew wealthier.

The Belgian administration also required Hutus to work on government projects meant to improve the colony. This labor, which was also enforced by Tutsi chiefs, drew the farmers away from the fields and threatened

In exchange for their services, the Tutsi oligarchy became members of an exclusive African bureaucracy that siphoned off surplus from the Africans below and maintained certain obligations and privileges as traditional authority figures.

their productivity. In one village of 2,024 people, for instance, 1,375 had to work on government projects each day. As the Belgian administration pressured the Tutsi chiefs to make the Hutu laborers work, they created a greater divide between the two groups. Rather than feeling animosity toward the Belgians, the Hutus grew to hate the Tutsi chiefs who enforced the harsh colonial policies.

Belgium's colonial policies highlighted the social differences between the Hutus and the Tutsis. The animosity grew even stronger when the Belgian administration declared that all people with 10 or fewer cows would be considered Hutus, and those with more than 10 would be classified as Tutsis. Identification cards stating each citizen's ethnic identity was the next step. The cards effectively turned Rwanda's pre-

viously flexible social divisions into rigid racial and ethnic divisions. An individual could not legally change his or her ethnic identity.

The Belgians favored the Tutsi aristocracy and conveyed this in a number of ways. By the early 1940s, this favoritism had created massive social changes. In precolonial times, Hutus and Tutsis had existed in a loose hierarchy that allowed for social movement and disregarded ethnicity. But Belgium's colonial policies created a society in which ethnicity determined a person's level of education, job, and standard of living. Tutsis, because of their ethnicity, held most of the wealth and the power. Hutus were considered inferior. The Tutsis, who believed they were the superior group, took advantage of these policies, while the Hutus became increasingly resentful.

BELGIANS MAKE CHANGES

The United Nations (UN), which replaced the League of Nations in 1945, made Ruanda-Urundi a trust territory in 1946. Belgium still had administrative authority in Rwanda, but was expected to make more social, educational, and political reforms. The Belgians had to modify the education system to enable more Hutus and disadvantaged Tutsis to gain some level of education. The UN also gave the Belgians a more detailed game plan for political reform in Rwanda, stating that Hutu and Tutsi citizens should share equal responsibilities in governing the territory. The Ten-Year Development Plan, established in 1952, crystallized these issues, calling for changes in social, political, and economic affairs.

The most significant changes were made by Belgian Catholic missionaries, many of whom had become opposed to the subjugation of the Hutus. In response to the calls for educational reform, Catholic mission schools started educating both Hutu and Tutsi children at the primary school level. By the 1950s, more Hutus were making their way through the system and becoming exposed to new ideas, some of which were eye-opening revelations. The concepts of democracy, freedom, and equality had a major impact on the Hutus, who began to look at their historic relationship with the Tutsis in new ways.

There were political changes as well. In 1952 the Belgian administrator decreed that, to broaden participation in the government, all Rwandan chiefs and subchiefs would be elected by the people, rather than appointed by the Belgian administration. By 1956 all adult men were given the right to vote, and a few Hutus rose to lower ranking government positions. Some Hutus became subchiefs. Even though Rwanda remained Tutsi dominated, the government reforms enabled a few Hutus to become involved in the colony's political process.

To balance power and wealth among Rwandan citizens, the Belgians dissolved the ubuhake system, which resulted in a redistribution of cattle among Hutus and Tutsis. The Tutsis remained in control of the land, however, so the Hutus still depended on them. After all, they needed land to graze their cattle. And, since land possession signified power, the Tutsis continued to dominate the Hutus. Therefore, these social changes merely highlighted the extent to which Hutus were still reliant on the Tutsis.

Although meant to satisfy the Hutu desire for equality, the Belgian reforms instead created an educated Hutu middle class that was dissatisfied with its role in Rwandan society. Educated Hutus believed that the changes made by the Belgians were insignificant. By the late 1950s, many educated Hutus were finding that they had few opportunities in the social and political arenas, which were still controlled by the Tutsi elite—who had no desire to give up their power. The few Hutus who were able to obtain positions of responsibility began demanding more changes and improvements in the social and political situation in Rwanda. To bring about real change, they believed they had to challenge the Tutsis.

THE GROWTH OF HUTU OPPOSITION

Two groups of educated Hutus contributed to the growing political equality movement in different ways. One group focused on breaking Tutsi social and political dominance. These Hutus were mainly interested in sharing power at the chiefdom and subchiefdom levels, not in overthrowing the monarchy. The other group, which believed sharing power was impossible, joined the priesthood and brought their anti-Tutsi feelings into rural areas throughout Rwanda.

Those in favor of political and social reform and power sharing were typically found in central and southern Rwanda. However, in northern Rwanda, where Hutu citizens had never fully supported the Tutsi monarchy, anti-Tutsi sentiment continued to grow. Uprisings in this region were based on ethnic hatred. The Hutus of this area, who had always resented Tutsi and European rule, wanted to completely eliminate these "foreigners" from Rwanda. Therefore, Rwanda had two anti-Tutsi movements brewing at the same time. They both had a similar aim—

The Role of the Catholic Church

During the late 1950s, the Roman Catholic Church played an instrumental role in helping the Hutus gain control of the country. Although early church leaders had favored the Tutsis, by the 1950s the rise of the Tutsi clergy was threatening the authority of Rwanda's Belgian Catholic priests. Many sympathized with the Hutus and used their influence to support the growth of the Hutu opposition. Belgian priests trained more Hutus for the priesthood and supplied Hutus with a sense of self-worth and new ideas about their right to equality.

The church also indirectly provided Hutus with financial support, making it possible for Hutu intellectuals to travel throughout Europe. During these trips, they explained their situation to influential people to gain political and financial support. In Rwanda, Hutu leaders such as Grégoire Kayibanda took over several church newspapers, which they used to voice their opinions about Tutsi oppression and to elicit more support from Belgian leaders and other Hutus.

Mwami Mutara III Rudahigwa with the archbishop of Belgium. The Belgian clergy initially favored the Tutsis and played a significant role in establishing Tutsi dominance. But in the 1950s, Belgian priests began to identify with the oppressed Hutu majority.

AP/Wide World Photos

Grégoire Kayibanda played a leading role in the Hutu opposition. While working as an editor for the Catholic newspaper Kinyamateka, Kayibanda gave voice to the rising anger of the Hutu middle class.

AP/Wide World Photos

to eliminate the dominance of the Tutsi minority.

With the support of the Catholic church, the Hutu opposition began challenging Tutsi dominance. Grégoire Kayibanda, a Hutu intellectual, and other Hutu leaders voiced their concerns about the social and political role of the Hutu community and about the uncompromising attitude of the Tutsi elite. In March 1957 Kayibanda and his supporters drew up the Manifesto of the Bahutu, a document that expressed a strong objection to the Tutsis social, political, and economic power. The document stated that it was unfair that the Tutsis, who accounted for only 15 percent of the Rwandan population, should control all aspects of society. The manifesto condemned prejudice against people because of their ethnicity and demanded more political opportunities for Hutus. The movement initiated by Kayibanda called for social and political reform and aimed to lead the country to a democratic, free, and equal society.

Meanwhile, the Tutsi elite was growing worried about Belgian reforms and the growth of Hutu opposition. They feared that they were going to lose their power. In response to these trends and to the Bahutu Manifesto, the High Council of State—a group consisting of Tutsi intellectuals and members of the Tutsi court—formulated its Statement of Views in 1957.

This statement outlined a plan to lead the country to independence and to establish a new government. The proposed government, however, would only include Tutsi politicians. The document stated that the relationship between Tutsis and Hutus should be one of patron and client and that Hutus could never share power with the Tutsis.

At this point, Tutsi dominance was still evident in Rwanda. By 1958 the Tutsis held 43 of 45 chiefdoms (the remaining two were vacant), 549 of 559 subchief positions, and 82 percent of the positions in the judiciary, agricultural, and veterinary systems. Equal representation of both ethnic groups in government became a major topic of conversation and debate. More and more Hutus began publicly voicing opinions against oppression and for equal representation. Hutu leaders expressed their views to the mwami and to the High Council but got little reaction. As a result, most Hutus became convinced that they would never be allowed to share power with the Tutsis.

By this time, the Belgians had begun to form new ideas about Rwanda too. The Belgians were angered that the Tutsis, whom they had supported and educated, were demanding independence. So the Belgian administration began to cultivate influence among educated Hutus by stating a new-found belief in the idea of democratic, majority rule. Tutsi leaders sensed that the changes signified a new attitude and that the Belgians were beginning to favor the Hutus.

TENSION INCREASES

During this period, many new political parties and organizations began forming to protest Tutsi dominance. These groups included the Association for the Social Betterment of the Masses (APROSOMA, in its French acronym), which condemned Tutsi domination, and the Ruandan Democratic Rally (RADER, in its French acronym), a group that supported democracy and improved ethnic relations. One of the largest and most influential groups was the Party of the Hutu Emancipation Movement (PARMEHUTU, in its French acronym). Led by Grégoire Kayibanda, this party claimed that it wanted to end Tutsi domination and the feudal system, as well as to give Hutus access to all levels of education. In response to these parties, Tutsi leaders established the Rwandan National Union Party (UNAR, in its French acronym), a promonarchy, anti-Belgian political organization that advocated immediate independence under Tutsi leadership.

The growing political activity heightened tensions in Rwanda. The Belgian administration prohibited political meetings and rallies to weaken the rising tensions and to avoid a potentially

The Hutu political movement, which stood to gain from majority rule—one of the governing concepts of decolonization at that time—was gaining momentum while segments of the Tutsi establishment resisted democratization and the loss of their acquired privileges.

A Tutsi chief asks a Belgian army officer for refuge. After the Hutu revolution had begun, Tutsi homes and property became a main target of the violence.

dangerous situation. Their efforts failed. In October 1959, UNAR supporters launched a campaign of intimidation against the Hutu opposition parties, leading to a final break between the Tutsis and the Belgian administration. Then, in November 1959, members of UNAR attacked a Hutu sub-chief who was also a member of PARMEHUTU. False rumors spread that the Hutu chief had been killed, and PARMEHUTU supporters retaliated by killing two members of UNAR. Over the next two weeks, riots and violence broke out across Rwanda. Groups of Tutsis attacked and killed members of PARMEHUTU and APROSOMA.

In response to these attacks, Hutus throughout the country looted and burned Tutsi homes, killed thousands of Tutsi civilians, and drove thousands more into neighboring countries. Decades of resentment boiled over into a surge of violence directed at the Tutsi minority. The Hutu revolution had begun.

CHAPTER

3

ENTRENCHED POSITIONS

Initially, the Belgians did not intervene to stop the violence that had engulfed Rwanda. They believed that such an upheaval was an unavoidable obstacle on the road to independence. But eventually the Belgians declared a state of emergency and put a curfew into effect. Then troops from Belgium and the Belgian Congo (named Zaire from 1971 to 1997 and later called the Democratic Republic of the Congo) arrived to stop the violence and to arrest the leaders who were instigating the fighting.

It soon became clear that the Belgians had completely switched allegiances and were on the side of the rebellious Hutus. Each time the Tutsis tried to fight back, the Belgians stopped them, enabling the Hutus to gain more power. Belgian favoritism became more obvious when

they arrested 919 Tutsis, as opposed to only 312 Hutus, for involvement in the fighting. The Belgian administration decided that UNAR supporters were responsible for much of the violence.

Fighting continued sporadically between the Hutus and the Tutsis throughout 1959 and into 1960, killing or driving from office 350 Tutsi chiefs and subchiefs. The Belgians helped the Hutus seize power by replacing these Tutsi leaders with Hutu politicians. The newly empowered Hutus continued to harass, kill, and drive away Tutsis. By the end of the spring of 1960, thousands of Tutsis were dead and about 22,000 Tutsis had been displaced. Many fled to government refugee centers in Rwanda, while others escaped to neighboring Burundi, Uganda, and the Belgian Congo.

TOWARD INDEPENDENCE

As the violence subsided, the Belgians took steps to resolve the territory's political problems. The Belgian administration began by turning the regions previously run by subchiefs into communes, with each commune having one leader and an elected council. Despite the opposition of the UN, which believed that it was first necessary to reconcile the Hutus and the Tutsis, the Belgians organized communal elections. These elections, the country's first, were held in mid-1960, and 2,390 out of 3,125 positions went to Hutu members of PARMEHUTU. Many Tutsis believed the election results were fraudulent, and UNAR officially boycotted the elections. Tutsi leader Mwami Kigeri, angry about the election process and the results, went to the

In 1960 Rwandans waited in line for their first opportunity to vote in communal elections. These elections resulted in a victory for the Hutus, who won the majority of positions in communal councils.

Belgian Congo to lodge a protest with UN officials. The Belgians decided not to let him back into the country.

The Belgians continued to overhaul the governmental structure. In late 1960, they established a 48-member provisional (temporary) government. This body elected Joseph Gitera—the head of APROSOMA—as president of the council of Rwanda and Grégoire Kayibanda as the prime minister of the provisional government. Belgian administrators then met with representatives of all Rwanda's political parties to discuss the Hutu-Tutsi conflict and the future of the territory. The biggest obstacle was the issue of the mwami. While Tutsi leaders wanted to maintain the monarchy, Hutu leaders wanted to abolish it. Because no progress was made at the meetings, the Belgians decided to delay the elections scheduled for January 1961. But to quell Hutu unrest over the stalled elections, the Belgian administration gave the provisional government self-governing powers.

In a move that challenged Belgian authority, Hutu leaders went forward with their own plans for the territory. At a meeting of the provisional government, the assembled Hutu leaders declared that the mwami and all symbols of Tutsi rule had to be eliminated. Gitera and Kayibanda created a new flag for Rwanda and declared the territory a republic. The new government also installed prefects around the territory. These prefects were administrators—similar to governors—who would be responsible for supporting democracy in their prefectures and for overseeing all political, administrative, economic, social, and cultural functions. The prefects would also maintain law and order in their respective regions. Rwanda was moving toward independence with or without Belgian consent.

A temporary legislative assembly, the lawmaking branch of the government, was then elected by the provisional government. A majority of this 44-person group included members of PARMEHUTU and APROSOMA. The UN,

which did not acknowledge the legitimacy of the provisional government, would not recognize the results. Belgian, UN, and Rwandan officials then met to discuss the leadership of Rwanda and, after unsuccessful negotiations, the Belgians assumed control of the country again. They set a new election date for September 1961, when the electorate would vote for members of the permanent legislative assembly and would decide on the structure of the Rwandan government.

The UN monitored the elections to ensure a fair outcome. The voters overwhelmingly favored Hutu

politicians, electing a legislative assembly that included 35 PARMEHUTU members, seven UNAR members, and two members from APROSOMA. When the legislative assembly took office the next month, its members voted to abolish the monarchy, to take away the powers of the mwami, and to establish Rwanda as a republic. These changes marked the end of monarchical rule in Rwanda.

Kayibanda became the first elected president of Rwanda, paving the way to freedom from Belgian rule. In June 1962, Rwanda's General Assembly voted to cut ties

Prior to legislative elections, United Nations officials held meetings to prepare people for the vote. The UN wanted to ensure that the elections would be fair and free of violence.

AP/Wide World Photos

with the Belgian administration, and the territory of Rwanda officially became the independent nation of Rwanda. (Urundi became the separate independent nation of Burundi at this time.) The new government exiled Tutsi leaders and UNAR supporters to Burundi.

Many Hutus considered Kayibanda one of the greatest men in Rwandan history. They believed he was a driving force in leading the nation to independence and in overthrowing the Tutsi monarchy. Kayibanda had asserted that the oppression of the Hutus was wrong and had convinced many Hutus to fight for their rights as equal citizens. The Belgians, who helped the Hutus gain power, were also viewed as heroes.

VIOLENCE AND DISCRIMINATION

Independence and the establishment of a new government did not end political violence in Rwanda. Fighting between the Hutus and the Tutsis continued. Members of the exiled UNAR party and other Tutsi refugees formed guerrilla groups called Inyenzi. The Inyenzi crossed into Rwanda from

In response to Tutsi guerrilla attacks, the Kayibanda government launched a wave of repression aimed at the Tutsis. Many Tutsi refugees ended up in Uganda, Burundi, and the Belgian Congo.

Burundi, Tanzania, Uganda, and the Belgian Congo to attack and kill Hutus and any Tutsi supporters of PARME-HUTU and the new government. Kayibanda's Hutu army, in turn, killed thousands of Tutsis still living in Rwanda. Between 1961 and 1966, the Inyenzi led 10 raids into Rwanda, each of which caused the government to retaliate against Rwanda's Tutsi minority. The largest of these assaults occurred in 1963, when the In-

yenzi attacked Bugesera and almost reached Kigali. After this attack, the military killed an estimated 10,000 Tutsis. Overall, the Rwandan army took the lives of about 20,000 Tutsi civilians during this period, including 20 Tutsi politicians. The violence perpetrated by the Rwandan government against the Tutsis also caused scores of Tutsi civilians to flee the country. By June 1962, there were already 120,000 Rwandan Tutsis in exile. By 1964 nearly 70 percent of Rwanda's Tutsis had fled the country. These exiled Tutsis became known as Banyarwanda.

The revolution that had initially begun as a social and political movement grew into an ethnic movement, in which the entire Tutsi population was targeted for political abuses by an elite group of Hutu leaders. Hutu dominance replaced Tutsi dominance. The social order in Rwanda had been completely upended. By 1964 Hutus were controlling the government, even though Tutsis still held some positions in education, in the government, and in religious spheres. The government discriminated against Tutsis in nearly all areas of society. Many Tutsis found themselves trying to change their ethnicity by obtaining new identity cards, while others sought protection from wealthy Hutus—a reverse of the old ubuhake system.

Things grew worse for the Tutsis in the late 1960s, when a Hutu extremist group from the region of Gitarama emerged and eventually took control of PARMEHUTU. The group tried to push Tutsis from their jobs and to bar them from living in Rwanda. The Gitarama group created conflict not only with the Tutsis, but also with other Hutu groups. While other Hutus were supportive of a multi-ethnic government and nation, the Gitarama group wanted to purge Rwanda of all Tutsis.

Rwanda and Burundi

Both populated by Hutus and Tutsis, Rwanda and Burundi have been linked throughout history. Events in Rwanda have often had an impact on Burundians and vice versa. In the precolonial era, a Tutsi monarchy ruled both countries. During the colonial era, which lasted until the second half of the twentieth century, they formed a single territory—Ruanda-Urundi. Nevertheless, when the nations gained independence, Rwandan and Burundian officials decided that Burundi and Rwanda should be separate countries, because political and social tensions had developed between the two regions over the years. Yet upheavals in these countries continue to impact both nations.

In many ways, Rwanda and Burundi are mirror images. Each country took a different path to independence. Rwanda gained independence through revolution, whereas Burundi achieved independence peacefully. After indepedence, a Hutu-led dictatorship ruled Rwanda, while Burundi was governed mostly by Tutsis. Each country holds different philosophies, viewpoints, and attitudes on how to deal with the Hutu-Tutsi conflict. While much of the violence in Rwanda since independence has been directed against the Tutsi minority by a Hutu government, the reverse is true in Burundi.

Although Burundi has not experienced Rwanda's level of violence, continuing conflict between Burundian Hutu and Burundian Tutsis has created instability. Burundi's Tutsi-led army has overthrown democratically elected Hutu leaders twice since 1993, fueling a backlash by Hutus. As in Rwanda, this struggle for power has led to bloodshed and human rights abuses, with civilians paying the heaviest price.

HABYARIMANA TAKES OVER

By the early 1970s, ethnic conflict and social discrimination had worsened under Kayibanda, whose policies alienated both Hutus and Tutsis. The hostility that the government showed toward the Tutsi minority created tension throughout the country. In addition, Rwanda was still a poor nation with few resources and a weak infrastructure. The Kayibanda government had done little to improve the economy and had become corrupt as well, keeping public money for the private use of its members. While those Hutus connected to the government benefited from the new social situation, conditions for the majority of the Rwandan people had not improved.

After a few years of relative peace, fighting between Hutus and Tutsis began again in 1973. This violence was inspired by the ethnic conflict that was flaring in neighboring Burundi at the same time and by a new round of anti-Tutsi discrimination that aimed to remove Tutsis from all educational and religious institutions. Many believed that Kayibanda, recognizing the waning popularity of his government, wanted to rekindle ethnic conflict to bolster his position. In response to this violence, the head of the Rwandan army—Major General Juvenal Habyarimana—and a group of northern Hutu military officers overthrew Kayibanda during a military **coup d'état.**

When he took over, Habyarimana announced that he would end ethnic politics and the divisive policies of the Kayibanda regime. Many Rwandans believed that the situation in the country would improve. But while Habyarimana did bring peace, it came at the expense of democracy. As the new president, Habyarimana eliminated the National Assembly, established martial (military) law, and dissolved the country's constitution. In 1975 he banned PARMEHUTU members from the government and eliminated all other political parties. The president asserted that his own new party, the National Revolutionary

AP/Wide World Photos

President Habyarimana met with French premier Pierre Messner in 1974. The French became significant supporters of the Habyarimana regime, providing financial aid and military support.

Movement for Development (MRND), would be the country's only political party. He filled government positions with family members and friends from his home region in northern Rwanda.

After winning the 1978 election (in which he was the only candidate) Habyarimana devised a new constitution, which formally stated that the MRND would be Rwanda's only political party. This meant that all prefects, commune leaders, and communal council members would have to be MRND members. In fact, every Rwandan citizen had to be a member of the MRND. Presidential elections would take place every five years. The general public was responsible for approving the president, who could serve an unlimited number of terms. The new system was essentially a dictatorship, in which Habyarimana and the MRND had total control over all military, political, and social activities.

Despite these authoritarian measures, there was hope that things would improve for Rwanda's Tutsis. In 1980 Habyarimana established the Equilibrium Policy—a plan to ensure that Hutus and Tutsis would have equal access to jobs and social positions across Rwanda. The policy stated that the government and the private sector would have to hire Hutus and Tutsis in accordance with their representation in the overall population. Therefore, if a company needed 100 workers, it would be required to hire about 85 Hutus and 14 Tutsis.

The policy, however, created resentment among Rwandan companies, which were sometimes required to hire unqualified Hutus or Tutsis just to make the numbers balance out. In addition, the policy was used by companies to exclude Tutsis from important positions. Although the situation for Tutsis was better than it had been under Kayibanda, Habyarimana was essentially continuing the country's discriminatory practices.

Another issue that created tension in Rwanda was the preference that the Habyarimana regime showed toward Hutus from the north. Because Habyarimana had come from this area, northerners were rewarded with jobs and other favors from the government. As a result, Hutus from the rest of Rwanda were discriminated against along with Tutsis.

THE REFUGEE PROBLEM

Habyarimana was reelected again in 1983 with no opposition. Under his rule, Rwanda remained relatively stable. In general, most Hutus and Tutsis got along. But while ethnic tensions had decreased under Habyarimana's regime, a serious refugee problem existed, stemming from the 1959 Hutu revolution and the attacks against Tutsis by the Kayibanda government in the 1960s and 1970s. By the early 1980s, more than 300,000 Rwandan Tutsis were living in exile. Most had fled to Burundi, but thousands were in Zaire, Uganda, and Tanzania. For many the

As the years passed and memories of the real Rwanda began to recede, Rwanda slowly became a mythical country in the refugees' minds.

refugee experience was difficult. While Tanzania and Burundi welcomed the Banyarwanda and respected their rights, Uganda and Zaire did not fully accept the refugees. Many Banyarwanda, even those who had been born in exile, yearned to return to Rwanda. Habyarimana refused to let them back into the country.

The most significant Tutsi refugee population—nearly 200,000—lived in Uganda. Because many had brought their cattle with them, the Banyarwanda in Uganda had been able to establish themselves socially and economically. By the early 1980s, however, many Ugandans had begun to resent the Tutsi exiles for taking much of their cattle-grazing land. This resentment turned to violence in 1983, when Ugandans—encouraged by the government of Ugandan president Milton Obote—attacked Banyarwanda communities. During this upheaval, up to 60,000 Banyarwanda were killed, and about 40,000 tried to go back to Rwanda. When the Rwandan government realized these refugees were trying to repatriate, it closed the

Yoweri Museveni, leader of Uganda's National Resistance Army, played a key role in organizing Uganda's Tutsi exiles into a united group.

border. About 4,000 were trapped in Uganda, while others fled to Tanzania.

The experience in Uganda fueled the desire of many Banyarwanda to return to Rwanda. Because there was no negotiating with the Habyarimana regime, many looked for a military solution to their problem. Then, in 1983, Yoweri Museveni, the minister of defense in

Uganda, recruited Rwandan Tutsi exiles to help organize the National Resistance Army (NRA), which aimed to overthrow President Obote. The Tutsi exiles, who were especially hostile to Obote after the 1983 persecutions, joined the NRA in large numbers and helped Museveni overthrow the government in 1986. In return for helping him, Museveni gave the Tutsi exiles weapons and a military base where they could train.

Eventually, the large number of Banyarwanda in the NRA became a problem for Museveni. Many Ugandans were still hostile to the Tutsi exiles, and Museveni began to distance himself from them.

At this point, Major General Fred Rwigyema and Major Paul Kagame, two Tutsi officers in the NRA, started to recruit Tutsi exiles for a force that could invade Rwanda and enable the Banyarwanda to return. This group formed the Rwandan Patriotic Front (RPF). A number of Hutu politicians who had grown disenchanted with the Habyarimana regime also joined the new organization.

The RPF was founded on eight principles—national unity, democracy, the creation of a self-sustaining economy, abolishment of political corruption, establishment of social services, democratization of security forces, progressive foreign policy, and an end to the system "that generates refugees." To obtain these goals, the RPF aimed to overthrow Habyarimana's government and to share power in Rwanda. Because Habyarimana had asserted throughout the 1980s that the Tutsi exiles would never be allowed to return to Rwanda, the RPF believed the only way the refugees would be able to go home was if they forced their way back into the country.

Meanwhile, the Rwandan government made no attempt to resolve the situation, and Tutsi exiles throughout the world criticized Habyarimana for his policy toward the Banyarwanda. Habyarimana continued to resist repatriation, claiming that the country was too overpopulated to withstand an increase in the number of residents, even if they were citizens in exile.

CALLS FOR CHANGE

In 1988 Habyarimana was reelected for a third time. But by this time, the cracks in his regime were affecting the country's stability. The refugee problem continued to be a divisive issue. In addition, the Rwandan economy had taken a severe downturn. Prices for coffee and tin, Rwanda's only exportable commodities, had collapsed. Land was scarce, and corruption within the government was becoming more pronounced. While government officials and MRND members pocketed export profits and foreign aid, the majority of Rwandans suffered. Lastly Habyarimana's policy of favoring northern Hutus was creating anger among southern Hutus and Tutsis.

Amid this turmoil, rumors were circulating that the RPF was preparing to attack Rwanda and overthrow the government. Adding to the tension within Rwanda were the growing number of people who were criticizing government corruption and calling for democratic reforms. These people included a number of human rights activists and journalists, many of whom were arrested and killed by the army. Students also began protesting and striking. Police, in turn, lashed out at students for their actions.

Facing page: *The ethnic problems that Rwanda has experienced are common to many countries in central Africa. Because colonial powers created borders that encompassed different kingdoms and peoples, many modern African nations include numerous ethnic groups that are often at odds with one another.*

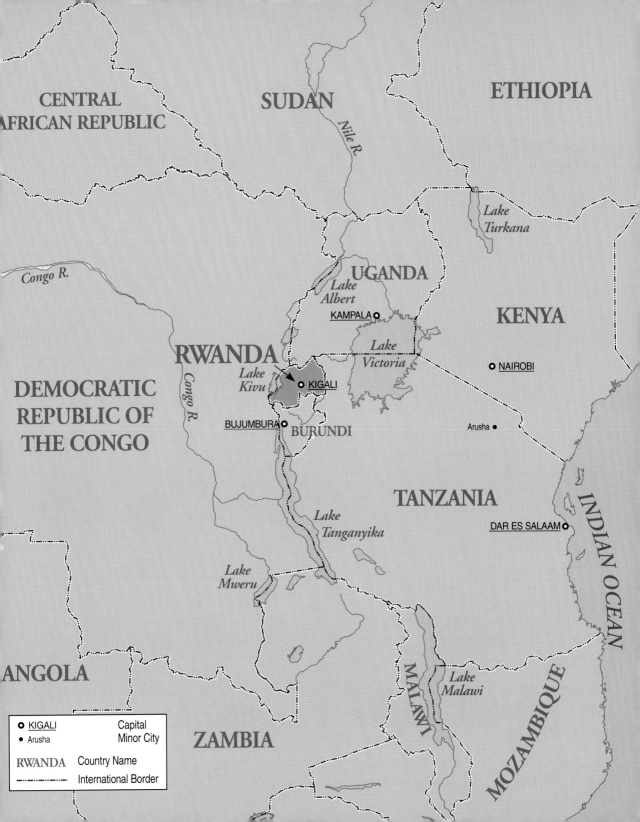

The Habyarimana government was still closely connected with Belgium, which not only provided Rwanda with large amounts of economic assistance but also controlled Rwanda's industries, including mining and manufacturing. In 1990, when Belgium and other foreign aid donors pressured Habyarimana to make social and political changes, he had to comply. Due to external and internal pressure, Habyarimana announced in July 1990 that he would allow Tutsi exiles to return to Rwanda and allow other political parties to form. Habyarimana further agreed to organize a multiethnic, democratic government that would include members of other parties. In addition, the president declared his intention to eliminate the country's national ethnic identity cards, which many people had stopped carrying out of fear of intimidation and personal harm. Despite his declarations, Habyarimana had little intention of making changes that would decrease his power.

THE RPF INVASION

Despite his claims, Habyarimana didn't take any major steps toward restructuring the government or repatriating the Tutsi exiles. As a result, Major Rwigyema led RPF forces from Uganda into northeastern Rwanda in 1990. The RPF raid killed 500 people and drove 350,000 more people, mainly Hutus, from their homes. But with the help of

AP/Wide World Photos

soldiers, weapons, and military advisers from Belgium, France, and Zaire, Habyarimana's government was able to rebuff the RPF forces in the northeast. The fighting stopped after several months, but the RPF continued to besiege Rwanda from its bases in Uganda throughout 1991 and 1992. During this period, neither side was able to gain the upper hand. A number of cease-fires were agreed upon and subsequently broken by both sides.

Facing Page: *RPF soldiers gather around an armored car taken from the Rwandan Armed Forces. Although the RPF invasion initially caught the Habyarimana regime by surprise, the conflict eventually turned into a stalemate.*

The RPF invasion coincided with the growth of political opposition to Habyarimana and the MRND. A number of new political parties had sprung up, including the Democratic Movement of Rwanda (MDR, in its French acronym), the Democratic Socialist Party (PSD, in its French acronym), the Liberal Party (PL, in its French acronym), and the Christian Democratic Party (PDC, in its French acronym). Although members of these groups held different attitudes toward the ethnic conflict and the RPF invasion, they all wanted to end one-party rule. Pressure for political change from these opposition groups and the international community forced the Habyarimana government—which had not yet fulfilled its promise to organize a new, multiparty government—to share leadership responsibilities. In 1992 the MRND formed a new government with members of the opposition. This government was supposed to rule until national elections took place in 1993.

Despite these concessions, President Habyarimana was determined to repulse the RPF invasion and to maintain his hold on the government. The government set about rapidly expanding FAR from 5,000 soldiers to 35,000. In addition, Habyarimana created the Presidential Guard, an armed force of soldiers recruited exclusively from his home district. Politically, Habyarimana made every attempt to divide the opposition, claiming that certain opposition members were RPF accomplices. The military arrested thousands of political opponents.

The president also unleashed a campaign of violence against Tutsi civilians. The armed forces were reported to have killed about 2,000 Tutsi civilians during a series of raids. According to the group Human Rights Watch, these people were killed because they were Tutsis. In addition, about 8,000 Tutsi civilians were jailed, tortured, raped, and beaten.

At the same time, a Hutu extremist movement was growing within the MRND and the military leadership. These Hutu extremists feared that they would lose their power if the RPF won the war. With the support of

Members of the Interahamwe, a militia group organized by the MRND, take part in a rally in support of president Habyarimana. Although the Interahamwe was originally intended to be a political youth group, it evolved into a violent militia that targeted opponents of the government.

Courtesy of Jean François Dupaquier and Association Memorial Internationale

Habyarimana, the MRND and an offshoot—the extremist Coalition for the Defense of the Republic (CDR)—recruited and trained Hutu youths to form a militia group that would fight the RPF and silence opponents of the government. This militia group helped the Rwandan military carry out the attacks against Tutsis and moderate Hutus around the country. The militia— known as the Interahamwe— also assassinated members of Hutu opposition parties, whom it believed were a threat to the government's power. Habyarimana and the extremists were determined to extinguish the RPF threat.

The Hutu extremists used pamphlets, newspapers, and radio broadcasts to stir up anti-Tutsi sentiment among the Hutu population. The propaganda reminded Hutus of past mistreatment by Tutsis and warned that the RPF planned a return to Tutsi dominance. In some areas, prefects and commune leaders—all of whom were MRND members—gathered residents together for education sessions in which they claimed that Tutsis and moderate Hutus were collaborating with the RPF and had to be attacked.

This type of propaganda created a climate of fear and tension among the Hutu population and played a central role in some of the anti-Tutsi attacks. For instance, in the town of Bugesera, a pamphlet warned that Tutsis in the area planned to rise up and attack their Hutu neighbors. Four months later, Interahamwe members and Hutu civilians killed more than 300 Tutsis in Bugesera. At other times, Hutu civil-

> *. . . as a result of the RPF attacks and a policy of deliberately targeted government propaganda, all Tutsis inside the country had been labeled accomplices to the RPF, and Hutu members of the opposition had been branded as traitors.*

ians stole food, slaughtered cattle, destroyed homes and crops, and attacked their Tutsi neighbors with machetes, clubs, and spears. During this period, many Tutsis fled the country.

STEPS TOWARD PEACE

After nearly two years of fighting, the RPF and the Rwandan government signed a cease-fire while meeting in Arusha, Tanzania, in July 1992. The cease-fire led to seven months of negotiations to come up with an agreeable plan for establishing a multi-party government. But in February 1993, the RPF violated the cease-fire and again attacked northeastern Rwanda, killing several hundred people, including civilians. The RPF claimed it broke the cease-fire in response to the slaughter of about 300 Tutsis in January by the Interahamwe militia. During the renewed fighting, hundreds

of civilians were killed and about 650,000 people fled their homes. A new cease-fire was put in place in March, but a Human Rights Watch report claimed that the RPF and the Rwandan government continually broke it. Meanwhile, negotiations between the warring parties continued.

In August 1993, the RPF and the Rwandan government finally signed a peace treaty, called the Arusha Peace Agreement. This peace accord laid out a plan to establish a power-sharing government—which would include opposition parties and RPF members—and a military consisting of FAR and RPF soldiers. The plan also outlined an agreement between the RPF and the Rwandan government to allow Tutsi exiles to repatriate and to help displaced citizens resettle. The UN, which was an official observer during

the peace talks, authorized the creation of a peacekeeping mission—the United Nations Assistance Mission to Rwanda (UNAMIR). The role of UNAMIR would be to help implement the peace agreement and to oversee the creation of a transitional government that would rule the country until democratic elections could be held. Faustin Twagiramungu, a Hutu member of the RPF, was chosen to be the prime minister of this transitional body. After three years of civil war, Rwanda seemed to be moving toward a peaceful solution to its problems.

Despite agreeing to the Arusha accords, Habyarimana was reluctant to give up power. Over the next few months, the president continued his efforts to divide the opposition parties, convincing some members to oppose the Arusha accords. Plans to implement the agreement were continually delayed, and by the end of 1993, hundreds of thousands of Rwandans were still displaced within the country or living in exile. Development of a transitional government was also stalled, as Rwanda's military and political leaders hedged on making changes. The government and CDR radio stations began broadcasting reports condemning Tutsis and Hutu moderates, increasing tension between the two groups.

At the same time, Hutu extremists within the Rwandan Armed Forces, the MRND, the CDR, and the Habyarimana government were also recruiting opposition members to oppose the accords. The extremists formed a "Hutu Power" faction intent on defeating the RPF and maintaining Hutu dominance. While the implementation of the new government was delayed, the extremists secretly stockpiled weapons to distribute to the Interahamwe militia. Attacks were launched against Tutsi civilians at the same time and a number of moderate opposition members were assasinated.

The Mysterious Death of the President

Although many theories abound, no one is certain who was responsible for firing the missiles that destroyed the plane carrying President Juvenal Habyarimana. One group of Hutu extremists claimed that Belgian UNAMIR soldiers fired the missile, based on an eyewitness account that described three white men running from the site where the missile was fired. Most members of the Rwandan government, however, believed that the missile attack was the work of the RPF, which controlled the area from which the missile came.

When the plane was shot down, the Presidential Guard quickly gained control of the airport and would not allow inspectors from the UN or any other group to examine the crash site to determine the cause of the accident. Many people believe this tight security served to hide evidence showing that Hutu extremists—with the help of the Rwandan Armed Forces and the Presidential Guard—shot down the president's plane and then blamed the RPF to rationalize the upcoming ethnic cleansing of Tutsis and moderate Hutus. The Hutu extremists' alleged motive was to stop the creation of a multiparty government and to impede implementation of the Arusha Peace Agreement. None of the theories about the plane crash, however, have been proven.

The growing extremist movement was turning against Habyarimana. The extremists feared that he would eventually give in to international demands to implement the Arusha agreement. Even though Habyarimana had supported their efforts, the extremists viewed him as a weak link. So they began to create a secret plan that would eliminate the political opposition and the Tutsi problem altogether.

As the stalling by the government and the opposition parties continued, the UN and the international commu-

In fact, although they pretended always to act in support of President Habyarimana and against his enemies, the CDR and the hardline faction of the MRND were increasingly taking an attitude of almost open defiance to their official leader.

After being hit by two missiles, President Habyarimana's jet crashed in the garden of his home, killing all aboard.

Presidential Guard, and the Interahamwe militias.

Some Hutu extremists blamed the president's death on the Belgians, who had pressured Habyarimana into accepting the Arusha accords. A Belgian peacekeeping force of 2,200 soldiers was in Rwanda at the time of the president's death to help enforce the peace accord. In response to Habyarimana's death, the Presidential Guard killed Agathe Uwilingiyamana, Rwanda's Hutu prime minister, and the 10 Belgian UN peacekeepers who were guarding her.

Much of the initial violence, which began in Kigali and spread throughout the country, was directed against Tutsis and the moderate Hutus who had supported the Arusha accords. Militia roadblocks appeared throughout Kigali to prevent people from leaving, and Interahamwe members went on house-to-house searches to locate those whom they believed were enemies. Using lists of names and addresses, they sought out and killed politicians, supporters of the opposition parties, journalists and priests who had criticized the government, and

nity pressured Habyarimana to install the new government. Regional leaders took it upon themselves to convince the Rwandan president to follow through with the Arusha Peace Agreement. On April 6, 1994, Habyarimana flew to Dar es Salaam, Tanzania, to meet with leaders from Tanzania, Kenya, Uganda, and Burundi. All urged the Rwandan president to implement the accords. On its way back to Kigali, the plane carrying Habyarimana and the president of Burundi was shot down by antiaircraft missiles. The plane crashed, and all aboard were killed.

THE CONFLICT ERUPTS

The death of the president immediately sent shock waves across Rwanda. Hutu extremists seized the moment. A flurry of violence ensued, launched by FAR soldiers, the

When the violence broke out, Interahamwe members and armed Hutu civilians attacked cars stopped at roadblocks (above) throughout Kigali, looking for Tutsis and moderate Hutus. Seeking shelter and safety from the violence, many Tutsis gathered in places such as the Sainte Famille Church in Kigali (left). Unfortunately, this site became the scene of a violent massacre.

civil rights activists. In fact, many of the victims in the capital were Hutus.

But as the violence spread beyond Kigali into the Rwandan countryside, it took on a predominantly anti-Tutsi nature. Most of the Hutu extremists accused RPF soldiers of firing the missile that destroyed the president's plane, and they used this accusation to justify retaliation against Rwanda's Tutsi population. The Interahamwe militia—along with FAR soldiers, members of the Presidential Guard, and communal police forces—began an organized, systematic slaughter of Tutsis. Throughout Rwanda prefects and commune officials organized and commanded Hutu civilians to assist the armed forces and the militias. Radio broadcasts encouraged the violence, urging Hutus to take up arms against the Tutsis.

For two days, chaos and violence reigned throughout the country. On April 8, FAR leaders organized the Committee of Public Salvation to form an interim government. The committee created a government that consisted mainly of extrem-

ists from the MRND and other Hutu opposition parties. Théodore Sindikubwabo, an MRND member, became president of the country and Jean Kambanda, an extremist from the MDR, took over

as prime minister. Their plan was to continue with the attacks against Tutsis and moderate Hutus while publicly calling for an end to the violence. Meanwhile, the killing continued.

Radio Rwanda

Before and during the violence of 1994, Hutu extremists within the MRND and CDR used various propaganda methods to encourage violence against Tutsis and moderate Hutus. Perhaps the most powerful means was the radio. In a country where nearly 60 percent of the population cannot read, radio transmissions were for many the only source of news and information.

Radio Rwanda is the main radio station in Rwanda, operated and funded by the government. Radio Rwanda journalists traditionally support the policies of the government. During the RPF invasion in 1990, Radio Rwanda repeatedly broadcast messages attacking the RPF and its motives while praising the government. With the signing of the Arusha accords and the growth of political opposition, however, the station took a more liberal stance and began criticizing the government. In response, CDR party members started an independent station, Radio Télévision Libre des Milles Collines (RTLMC). Devoted to the cause of Hutu power and opposed to the Arusha Peace Agreement, RTLMC provided a platform for extremist politicians and journalists to criticize the political opposition and to denounce the RPF and its supporters. RTLMC became known for spreading rumors to incite violence.

In 1994 Hutu extremists used both stations to create a climate of hysteria, warning people about the RPF and urging them to pick up weapons and fight. Songs and poems glorifying anti-Tutsi violence mixed with speeches reminding Hutus to complete the unfinished business of the 1959 revolution. After the RPF victory, both stations urged Hutus to flee the country.

THE PRESENT CONFLICT

On April 9, 1994, the RPF officially resumed hostilities with the Rwandan government. RPF troops came down from the north and by April 11 had reached Kigali, where a battalion of 600 troops was under siege. The next day, the interim government fled to Gitarama, while the government radio station urged Hutus to defend the country against the RPF invaders. RPF leaders said they would only stop fighting once they had driven away the Hutu extremists, established a multiparty government, and arrested those responsible for the killings of Tutsis and moderate Hutus.

Meanwhile, widespread violence continued throughout the country. By the end of April, UN officials estimated that militia members, soldiers, and civilians had killed nearly 200,000 Tutsis and moderate Hutus. Despite the international community's awareness of the killing, little was done to stop it. The UNAMIR forces were too small and lightly armed to stop the militia members and FAR soldiers. In fact many of the killings committed by soldiers and militia members occurred in front of UN soldiers. Fearing for the safety of these troops, the UN voted in late April to cut UNAMIR forces by 90 percent. In May the UN authorized the deployment of an intervention

RPF soldiers load weapons and ammunition onto a truck. Soon after the violence began, the RPF unleashed a massive counterattack to overthrow the interim government.

When it became clear that the RPF was going to win the war, Hutu civilians started packing up their belongings and fleeing the country.

force—UNAMIR II—to end the fighting in Rwanda, but by this point, the RPF claimed, the time for UN intervention had passed.

As the RPF gained territory in northern Rwanda, scores of Hutu civilians fled into Zaire, Burundi, and Tanzania. While many of these civilians feared that RPF troops would kill them in retaliation, they were also urged to leave by the same people who had instigated and organized the violence. Local authorities and Interahamwe members intentionally told Hutu civilians to flee, warning them that they would be slaughtered if they stayed.

By May the RPF had gained the upper hand, spurring an ever-larger exodus of Hutu refugees, who believed they would be killed by the advancing forces. The fighting in Kigali was still intense, but elsewhere FAR soldiers and militia members did not put up much of a fight. During this time, the RPF began taking in new members—many of whose relatives had been killed by the militias—for a final assault on Kigali. Some of these new recruits were eager to retaliate against Hutus and committed atrocities against civilians. This was a blow to the reputation of the RPF, which had been extremely well disciplined.

RPF leaders did not want the international community to view the situation in Rwanda as one in which both sides were to blame.

In late June, France sent a force of 2,500 troops to help stop the violence and chaos along the Zaire-Rwanda border, as well as to prevent millions of Rwandans from fleeing the country. The French created a neutral zone in southwestern Rwanda that drew thousands of refugees. The interim government welcomed the intervention and hoped that the French—who had supported the Habyarimana regime and had helped train FAR soldiers—would help

An RPF soldier guards Hutus accused of being Interahamwe members (left). *After the RPF victory, Major General Paul Kagame* (below) *became the vice president of the country.*

fight the RPF. The RPF distrusted the French intervention, believing that the French troops would try to bolster the interim government. Despite the conflicting expectations, the French forces remained neutral.

On July 4, 1994, the RPF took Kigali, fueling the flight of nearly three million people—civilians, soldiers, militia members, and local authorities—toward the French neutral zone and the Zairian border. By July 14, the RPF had conquered Butare and the interim-

government stronghold of Ruhengeri. By July 17, the RPF had reached the border of Zaire and was in control of the entire country, except for the French neutral zone. A cease-fire went into effect July 17, 1994, and the victorious RPF rebels declared an end to the war.

POSTWAR PROBLEMS

After they had won the war, the victorious RPF immediately set about installing a new government. Pasteur Bizimungu—a moderate Hutu and one of the top figures in

the RPF—was inaugurated as president. Major General Paul Kagame, a Tutsi, was made vice president and defense minister, and Faustin Twagiramungu was named prime minister. This new government—called the Broad Based Government of National Unity—included political leaders from Rwanda's opposition parties and followed the directions laid out in the 1993 Arusha Peace Agreement. Of the 20 other cabinet members sworn into office, five were RPF leaders.

"Today is a day of joy and sorrow," said Kagame in his inauguration speech. "The (rebel) army has removed a system of oppression and dictatorship but only at the cost of many lives."

Although the mass killings of Tutsis and moderate Hutus had ended, the RPF's military victory did not immediately solve Rwanda's problems. The number of people fleeing Rwanda had created a humanitarian crisis that none of the region's countries were able to handle. The UN and other aid organizations had established refugee camps in Zaire, Burundi, and Tanzania, but the camps were poorly equipped and were overflowing with people. A massive refugee problem also existed within Rwanda, where hundreds of thousands were displaced from

their homes. Many people were still hiding in the hills, fearing a return of the militias. Those who had survived the violence were in a state of shock. Much of the nation's infrastructure had been destroyed.

By August 1994, new problems with the refugee situation had become clear. Not all the refugees were innocent victims of the civil war. Interahamwe members and FAR soldiers had also ended up in the refugee camps, where they were treated for wounds, fed, and nursed back to health by NGO workers. (NGOs typ-

ically give aid to anyone in need and don't discriminate against people because of their ethnicity or political beliefs and actions.) As a result, military personnel and militia members were as likely to be fed and cared for as mothers and children with no political affiliation. This policy enabled the Hutu extremists to recuperate and regroup in the refugee camps.

Although run by NGOs and international aid organizations, many of the refugee camps ended up under the control of the armed militia members, who intimidated and threatened those who

Refugees unload food and supplies at a camp in Zaire. In many camps, Hutu militia members and commune leaders who had instigated violence ended up in charge of distributing supplies.

considered returning to Rwanda. They told refugees that the Tutsis would kill them if they tried to return to their homes. Often, they made up stories about people who had supposedly returned home and were tortured or killed upon their arrival. Because the refugees had only a limited amount of information about the situation and often didn't know what story to believe, they were afraid to go home. They feared that if they repatriated, the RPF would retaliate and kill them.

NGO workers, who were unarmed, could do nothing to prevent the armed extremists from controlling the camps. As a result, the extremists managed to gain control of aid supplied by NGOs. In some cases, village leaders who had helped organize the killing of Tutsis were in charge of distributing food in the refugee camps. In addition, the militias set up military training camps in eastern Zaire and on

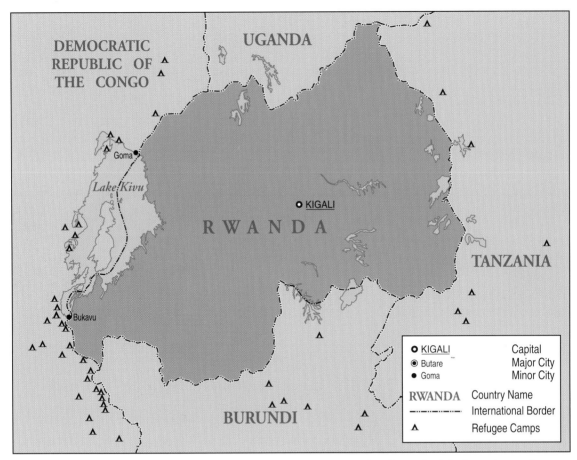

This map shows the locations of the refugee camps that sprouted up in the aftermath of the Rwandan civil war.

The Reaction of the International Community

Since the end of the civil war, the Rwandan government has sharply criticized the UN and the international community for their reactions to the 1994 violence. Months before the death of President Habyarimana, UNAMIR learned from sources inside Rwanda that Interahamwe members were gathering weapons and planning to kill large numbers of Tutsis and moderate Hutus. Although UNAMIR commanders warned the Rwandan government and the staffs of the U.S. and Belgian embassies about this plot, nothing was done to prevent it. UNAMIR stated that intervening in the situation was beyond its stated mission and might create unnecessary violence.

When the civil war resumed in April, UNAMIR forces provided aid to the wounded but could not protect those being attacked by the Hutu militias. French and Belgian soldiers *(above)* were sent to Kigali but only to remove their own embassy workers and officials. They offered little assistance to the thousands of scared Rwandans. The U.S. government, which was opposed to sending its own troops to Rwanda, argued that the killings were the result of fighting between FAR and the RPF. A few NGOs were able to help the injured, but their presence was small and they could not prevent the killing. When French troops established a neutral zone, RPF leaders argued that it provided a safe haven for FAR soldiers and Hutu militia members.

RPF leaders were further angered by the attention given to the refugee crisis, because little mention was made of the massacres that had preceded it. The United States led a large effort to get humanitarian supplies to the refugee camps. Widespread coverage of this crisis in the news caught the attention of the world, leading to an outpouring of support for the Rwandan refugees. But the existence of the camps allowed the people who had organized the violence to reorganize and instigate new rounds of violence. In recent years, international leaders—including U.S. president Bill Clinton—have apologized to Rwanda for their failure to act.

the outskirts of refugee camps. After the war, Zairian camps were believed to hold as many as 10,000 militia members and 30,000 FAR soldiers.

Although much of the propaganda spread by the Hutu extremists was false, the situation in Rwanda for returning refugees did contain dangers. Cases of RPF soldiers retaliating against Hutu civilians existed throughout the country. There was also the problem of the Tutsi exiles returning to Rwanda from Burundi, Zaire, Uganda, and Tanzania on the heels of the RPF victory. By August more than 200,000 Banyarwanda had gone back to Rwanda. Upon their return, they claimed property that had been abandoned during the

Soon after the RPF victory, Tutsi exiles began rapidly returning to Rwanda. Many needed government assistance to find new homes. Some families assumed ownership of land and property abandoned by fleeing Hutus.

RPF advance. Some accused the RPF leadership of turning a blind eye to this confiscation of property.

By late 1994, the Hutu militias were crossing the border into Rwanda from Zaire and Tanzania on a regular basis, sparking clashes with the newly created Rwandan Patriotic Army (RPA)—an army that included RPF troops and former FAR members who had been retrained. These infiltrations led to new rounds of violence against Hutu civilians by the RPA, which be-

lieved that some Hutus were aiding the militias. UN observers noted that kidnappings, executions, and destruction of property were taking place throughout Rwanda. The government denied that the army's actions were part of a deliberate policy of retaliation.

Despite the government's claims, the RPA was involved in numerous cases of anti-Hutu violence. In April 1995, according to the United Nations High Commissioner for Refugees (UNHCR), RPA troops killed between 2,000

and 4,000 people when they tried to close the Kibeho displaced persons' camp—which the government believed was under the control of Hutu extremists. During one of several days of chaos, RPA troops allegedly fired gunshots into the air to force the 250,000 refugees out of the area. When the scared refugees began to run, the troops fired at the crowds, later claiming they did this out of self-defense. However, the international aid agency Médecins Sans Frontières (Doctors Without

Borders) reported that many Hutus were shot in their backs as they ran away from the RPA troops. Incidents like these were detrimental to relations between the Hutus and the Tutsis, as well as to the overall peace process.

Political problems also grew for the RPF. The ministerial seats in the new government were meant to be split equally among the RPF and the opposition parties. But the RPF had taken the seats allocated to the MRND, whose members had fled the country. By taking these extra seats, the RPF controlled the government. The opposition parties were opposed to the amount of power held by the RPF in the new government, and the international community called on the RPF to broaden the government's political base.

RETURNING THE REFUGEES

By mid-1995, the refugee situation remained the most pressing issue for Rwanda. The UNHCR and the United States Committee for Refugees (USCR) proposed that one of the first steps to repatriating refugees was arresting the thousands of Hutu extremists who were pre-

> *"It was all lies. . . . The Hutu soldiers said if we return to Rwanda, [the Tutsis] will kill us. I'm not afraid of going back to Rwanda."*
>
> A Hutu Refugee

venting people from returning home. Propaganda circulating in the camps had become one of the most harmful obstacles in the repatriation process. Refugees in the camps didn't know who to believe or what information was accurate. They often disregarded positive news, because they thought reports about refugees who had repatriated without being harmed were a form of entrapment by the new government to lure people home. Many still believed they would be killed upon their return.

To eliminate some of these fears and to help the refugees feel more secure, the USCR recommended the construction of a new radio station for broadcasting accurate and positive information. Broadcasts would include current information regarding conditions within Rwanda, as well as reports about refugees who had been welcomed home unharmed. These reports would also contain information about Rwanda's judicial system, about human rights, about relief and development projects, and about guidelines for reclaiming property. By October 1995, the UNHCR branch in Goma was working with Radio Agatashya in Zaire to broadcast information to refugees. Because many NGO workers also lacked up-to-date information, the USCR provided NGOs with accurate information, so that aid workers could help dispel myths and eliminate propaganda.

The UN group used several tactics to convince refugees to return home. To stimulate voluntary repatriation, the UNHCR intentionally tried to make living conditions worse in the refugee camps. They closed numerous facilities, such as restaurants and bars, and put a halt to fixing up the camps. They requested that NGOs stop building new toilets, schools, and other facilities. The UNHCR also banned

CHAPTER 4 *The Present Conflict*

refugees from setting up homes or businesses outside the camps and forbade them from getting jobs in Goma by barring them from the township area.

Rwandan president Pasteur Bizimungu claimed that he supported the return of the refugees. In a speech in September 1995, according to the UNHCR, Bizimungu said he would welcome the refugees home. He also stated that the government "reiterates its determination to do everything possible to enable the return of Rwandan refugees. No efforts will be spared to ensure that every Rwandan enjoys equal rights to citizenship and protection by the government."

But it was clear that Rwanda needed the help of leaders from the region to speed up the repatriation process. On November 19, 1995, former U.S. president Jimmy Carter met with leaders from Burundi, Rwanda, Zaire, and Uganda in Cairo, Egypt, where they signed an agreement to repatriate Rwandans from camps in Zaire and Tanzania. One of the biggest obstacles in alleviating the Hutu-Tutsi conflict, the leaders agreed, was figuring out a way to bring these refugees home without causing more violence.

In the agreement, the Rwandan government ensured that no refugees would be harmed upon their return. The government also said that it would do as much as possible to help refugees reclaim their property, much of which had been confiscated by Rwandan Tutsis and by Tutsi exiles who had returned to the country. The agreement outlined a plan for repatriating as many as 10,000 refugees a day.

The decision to bring Rwandan refugees home came just one month and several days before a planned repatriation of the refugees by Zaire. President Mobutu Sese Seko of Zaire had announced that on December 31, 1995, he would begin closing camps and forcing refugees in Zaire back to Rwanda. NGO workers feared that pressure by Zairian troops would lead to violence, killing, and chaos. They believed that the best tactic for bringing the refugees home was through a monitored, organized program administered by the

Former U.S. president Jimmy Carter accepts a gift from a Rwandan refugee. Carter played an instrumental role in efforts to encourage the refugees to return to Rwanda.

Reuters/Corinne Dufka/Archive Photos

Refugees in Zaire

The presence of large numbers of Rwandan refugees had a huge impact on eastern Zaire, particularly the town of Goma. As some refugees assimilated into Zairian culture, they drained the jobs and land that Zairians claimed belong to that country's citizens. The refugees stripped Goma of most of its trees, which they used for firewood and making homes. In addition, due to the lack of proper sewage facilities in the camps, the soil and water in the area became polluted. The refugee presence also led to severe overcrowding in Goma. To draw refugees away from Goma, aid agencies set up four camps between 10 and 40 miles outside of the town.

On the other hand, the refugee situation was in some ways beneficial for many Zairian officials and soldiers, who made money from having the refugees and aid agencies in their country. Zairian officials continually confiscated NGO automobiles for little or no reason and returned them after a "fine" had been paid. Zairian airport personnel also frequently taxed incoming and outgoing airplanes carrying lifesaving medical supplies.

East African governments and the UN or through voluntary repatriation.

OBSTACLES

Despite these efforts, little repatriation had taken place by the spring of 1996. The Rwandan government, although publicly supportive of repatriation, was divided over how to handle the situation. Tutsi extremists in the RPF wanted to keep the refugees out and to build a new Tutsi kingdom. The more moderate government officials believed that the refugees should be allowed to return. Most agreed that the camps needed to close down to force out the Hutu militias. Yet they also feared that repatriation would bring the militias back into the country.

The Hutu militias continued to pose a threat, attacking Tutsis and supporters of the new Rwandan government from their bases within the refugee camps. The militias believed they could only return to Rwanda by toppling the RPF government, regaining control, and eliminating the Tutsis. According to Human Rights Watch, Colonel Théoneste Bagasora, an official of the ousted Rwandan government, claimed that his group planned to "wage a war that will be long and full of dead people until the minority Tutsi are finished and completely out of the country."

This attitude only reflected the views of a select group of people, however. Not all Hutu leaders or civilians felt this way. Others believed the Hutus would be defeated in another military battle. Many wanted to return peacefully to Rwanda and reestablish the old "democratic" government that existed before the war. These people were supportive of a power-sharing government, but one in which the majority—the Hutu ethnic group—ruled.

The most significant obstacle remained the refugees' fear of returning to Rwanda. To reassure and protect refugees during repatriation, Carter and the four African leaders who met in Cairo requested that UNAMIR II forces remain in Rwanda. The UN also placed more than 100 human rights field monitors throughout Rwanda to monitor relations among people and to ensure peace between Hutus and Tutsis. In addition, these field monitors would work with Rwandans, from civilians to military officials, on human rights issues. Other countries and organizations, such as the European Union, sent human rights monitors to Rwanda as well.

The consensus among refugees who had safely returned to Rwanda was that all refugees should repatriate. There were many stories about people who had repatriated without harm. In many cases, people were welcomed back into their communities by both Hutus and Tutsis. To help ease the repatriation process, the USCR recommended that the government devise a solution for resettling Banyarwanda, as well as civil war refugees, upon their return.

PROBLEMS IN ZAIRE

The refugee situation worsened in October 1996, when Laurent Kabila of Zaire began a rebellion aimed at purging Rwandan refugees from Zaire. Kabila had organized an army, called the Alliance of Democratic Forces for the Liberation of Congo-Zaire, which included a large number of Zairian Tutsis. The Rwandan government, which publicly denied any connection to the Zairian rebels, supported this military action with troops and supplies. In fact, about nine months after the start of the rebellion, Rwanda's vice president and defense minister Paul Kagame admitted that the Rwandan government had planned and directed the rebellion, hoping that it would end the refugee problem. Eventually, the uprising grew into a national rebellion to oust President Mobutu.

Kabila wanted to drive the Rwandan refugees out of Zaire because he believed that the Hutu militias in the

Ethnic Conflict in Zaire

The uprising in Zaire in 1996 arose from ethnic problems in eastern Zaire. The Banyamulenge are Zairian Tutsis who have lived in the region for nearly 200 years. Many of the Banyamulenge are wealthy, and their success has spurred resentment among other ethnic groups in eastern Zaire. By mid-1996, Zairian leaders and Hutu militia members in the Rwandan refugee camps were encouraging this resentment to spur violence against the Banyamulenge. Then, in October 1996, the Zairian authorities ordered nearly 400,000 Banyamulenge to leave the region. But the Rwandan army, concerned about the Hutu extremists in the refugee camps, had secretly been arming and training Banyamulenge militias, which rebelled against the Zairian orders. At the same time, the Rwandan military launched cross-border raids into the refugee camps in Zaire to remove Hutu militia members. This conflict, once again pitting Hutu against Tutsi, became the starting point of the Zairian revolution.

These events underscore the impact of the Hutu-Tutsi conflict in central Africa. With Hutus and Tutsis living in Burundi, Zaire, Tanzania, and Uganda, fighting in one area can affect all the nations of the region, adding fuel to long-simmering ethnic tensions.

Reuters/Peter Andrews/Archive Photos

On the move once again, refugees head back to Rwanda after being forcibly removed from camps in Zaire.

refugee camps were being armed by the Zairian government to help President Mobutu retain power. In addition, the militias had been involved in attacks on Zairian Tutsis. The conflict ended up pitting Kabila and his Tutsi allies, including the Rwandan government forces, against Mobutu, his Zairian troops, and their Hutu allies, including Rwanda's Hutu militias. Kabila stated that if the refugees didn't leave, his army would forcibly remove them from the camps.

In October 1996, Kabila's forces, with the help of Zairian villagers who also wanted to get rid of the refugees, attacked camps in eastern Zaire. During the attack, more than 100,000 Hutu refugees fled into Zaire's forests and mountains, because they didn't want to be sent back to Rwanda. Kabila's forces fol-lowed the fleeing refugees into the forests, killing thousands. Nearly 100,000 people were still unaccounted for a year later. In November Kabila ordered a cease-fire to allow refugees to return to Rwanda. But as refugees began repatriating, Kabila's forces raided the Mugunga refugee camp in Goma to kill Hutu militia members. This military action created chaos and sparked a massive return of refugees to Rwanda.

By November 17, nearly 250,000 Rwandans had returned home. Another 250,000 people repatriated over the next four days. (Kabila eventually ousted President Mobutu and renamed Zaire the Democratic Republic of the Congo in May 1997.)

Some of the refugees were forced to return home at gunpoint by the Zairian rebels. Others were happy to be going back to Rwanda and escaping the grip of the Hutu militias. Rwandan president Bizimungu was at one of the border crossings with a megaphone, welcoming the refugees back to Rwanda. For the Rwandan government, the closing of the camps and the return of the refugees meant that the Hutu militias would no longer have bases from which to launch attacks. A month later, another 500,000 refugees returned to Rwanda from Tanzania, where they were forced out by the government. By early 1997, 1.3 million refugees had returned to Rwanda.

MORE VIOLENCE

Although the Rwandan government believed that the return of more than one million refugees from Zaire and Tanzania would help the country get back on its feet, the violence in Rwanda continued. While some clashes occurred between Hutu and Tutsi civilians, most of the fighting involved the RPA and the remnants of the Hutu militias, which continued to launch raids in northwestern Rwanda. Thousands of civilians were caught in the middle of this fighting. It is estimated that between May and July 1997, more than 2,300 people—unarmed men, women, and children—were killed in northwestern Rwanda. By September 1997, more than 6,000 civilians had been killed in the violence.

The Hutu insurgents, despite their disorganization, regularly attacked and killed RPA troops, Tutsi civilians, and Hutus whom they feared sympathized with the Rwandan government. In December 1997, for instance, Hutu militias killed 300 Tutsi refugees in the Mudende refugee camp in northwestern Rwanda. The insurgents also attacked people who might have been able to testify about crimes committed in 1994. Most of these attacks had no military objective, but were a continuation of the ethnically motivated violence of 1994. In addition, the Hutu insurgents repeatedly attempted to create friction between Hutu civilians and the RPA.

The RPA also attacked civilians and committed numerous human rights violations. RPA soldiers killed several Hutu civilians while on armed missions to find Hutu insurgents. Local authorities and Tutsi civilians also helped RPA soldiers track down Hutu civilians whom they either believed to be a threat or believed to have committed a crime against a Tutsi in the past. Throughout 1997 and 1998, RPA soldiers kidnapped, tortured, and killed thousands of unarmed civilians. According to Amnesty International, more civilians were killed by the RPA in 1997 than by Hutu insurgents. Some of this violence occurred during security sweeps by the RPA. Other times, the killings were perpetrated for political reasons or out of revenge. Many attacks went unreported or were covered up by civilians, the RPA, or the government. ⊕

Gorillas in the Mist

In the middle of a lush tropical rain forest that spreads across Rwanda, Zaire, and Uganda live the world's only mountain gorillas *(Gorilla beringei)*. About 310 to 320 mountain gorillas inhabit the Mgahinga Gorilla National Park in Uganda, the Volcanoes National Park in Rwanda, and the Virunga National Park in Zaire.

The mountain gorilla is on the world's endangered species list. The gorillas were once targets for poachers, who sold the animals' hands and heads to collectors, and for local government officials, who sometimes captured gorillas to sell to zoos. (Throughout the 1970s and early 1980s, the Rwandan government believed that the sale of one mountain gorilla to a zoo could provide much-needed food, clothing, and medicine for the region's citizens.) Fewer gorillas would have survived had it not been for the work of several researchers, including Dian Fossey, an American researcher who spent about 13 years in Rwanda studying and protecting the species. Fossey, however, was killed mysteriously in 1985. Her story became the basis of the movie *Gorillas in the Mist.*

By the late 1980s, gorilla tours in Rwanda's Virunga Mountains had become popular, providing millions of dollars for the nation's economy. Because the economy would suffer if Rwanda lost its gorillas, no gorillas were killed or captured for a number of years. But in the early 1990s, the gorilla population felt the impact of the Rwandan conflict. Militia members and soldiers brought more advanced fighting equipment into gorilla territory. In 1992 Rwandan soldiers killed the head male gorilla—called the silverback—in one group. Normally, human trackers kept watch over and protected the mountain gorillas. When the civil war began, however, most trackers and park service staff were either killed or evacuated.

After the civil war ended, the mountain gorilla remained in danger. According to the Kenya branch of the International Gorilla Conservation Program, poachers or soldiers killed at least eight gorillas in Uganda and Zaire in 1995. Other animal protection groups claimed that poachers were still hunting the gorillas for their meat. Conservationists worried that the killings might jeopardize the trust that had developed between gorillas and humans during the 30 years before the civil war.

Another concern of conservationists was that Rwandan refugees were cutting through the gorillas' territory as they fled to Zaire, destroying sections of the gorillas' habitat. In addition, refugees camped along the edge of the Virunga Mountains tore down trees from the rain forest to build shelters and to use as firewood. Within a year after the war began, refugees had cleared several square miles of forest.

There was also concern that the shortage of food in Rwanda could affect the gorillas. By the end of 1995, many of Rwanda's crops had died or been eaten and much of the country's livestock and poultry had been consumed. Conservationists were concerned that the food shortage might encourage refugees to hunt wild animals and that the mountain gorillas could be caught in their traps. The Rwandan government has said that it supports efforts by conservation groups to protect the gorillas, and the population has begun to rebound since the end of the war.

CHAPTER 5

WHAT'S BEING DONE TO SOLVE THE PROBLEM

Despite continuing violence, many aspects of life in Rwanda are getting back to normal. Restaurants and bars have reopened, the markets are regularly supplied with produce and goods, and commerce is thriving. Towns and villages throughout the country are once again brimming with activity. The government has cleaned up the bombed-out and stripped-down cars that once lined streets of the capital.

But reminders of the civil war are everywhere. The roads and many buildings in Kigali are pockmarked with mortar holes. Homes in Kigali and across the country lie in ruins. Many are completely bombed out, while others are missing roofs and sit abandoned.

Children at the primary and secondary levels have gone back to school. One of the first lessons that teachers presented was how to avoid the land mines that are still scattered around the country. Teachers have also had to nurture children who had witnessed some of the horrors of the war, such as seeing friends and family members tortured and killed. These images have traumatized many Rwandan children.

Rwanda's only public university, Université Nationale du Rwanda, with campuses in Butare and Ruhengeri, has reopened. The country's newspapers, which had stopped printing during the war, are publishing again, and the government-operated Radio Rwanda is on the air. The radio station had been used as a propaganda tool during the civil war, when the government aired regular broadcasts urging Hutus to commit acts of violence against Tutsis. But since the war, Radio Rwanda has become a propaganda tool for the new government, with hourly broadcasts encouraging refugees to return to Rwanda. Recently, Radio Rwanda has been expanded to include broadcasts from international stations.

Despite these hopeful signs, Rwanda still has a long way to go. Although the government is trying to focus on the economic and structural rehabilitation of the country, the ethnic and political struggle continues to dominate the headlines. Furthermore, Rwanda's citizens—Hutu and Tutsi alike—have been trau-

At an overcrowded prison in Kigali, Hutu men arrested for taking part in the violence of 1994 await sentencing. Some prisoners have waited years for a trial.

matized by the extreme violence that occurred in 1994. People have lost family members, friends, homes, and possessions. Some Rwandans still live in fear because, in many cases, the violence was perpetrated by friends and neighbors. With the refugees of 1994 returning, victims of the violence are being asked to forgive those who tried to harm them. At the same time, refugees who played no part in the violence are viewed suspiciously by their neighbors. The ethnic divide in Rwanda has grown wider.

Since the end of the war two of Rwanda's leading problems have been prosecuting those responsible for the killings committed in 1994 and peacefully repatriating the approximately two million refugees who fled the country in the wake of the RPF victory. The Rwandan government must find a way to balance the Tutsi minority's anger and desire for justice with the fears of the Hutu majority. These are challenging, long-term tasks that demand a large amount of planning, resources, and negotiations.

PROSECUTING THE GUILTY

After the war, arresting the people involved in the mass killings of Tutsis and moderate Hutus became one of the main issues of concern for RPF leaders, who believed that justice would be the first step in the reconciliation process. The new government arrested more than 60,000 people—mainly civilians—in Rwanda within a year after the end of the war. In April 1995 alone, the government arrested about 7,000 people for war-related crimes. But prosecuting those arrested turned out to

Prison Conditions

The Rwandan government's desire for justice has put great strain on the country's prison system. The Gitarama Prison, for instance, was built to hold 600 people, but by 1995 it was jam-packed with nearly 7,000 prisoners. Most of these prisoners were held in an outer courtyard, exposed to the hot sun and torrential rains. Before the situation improved, people in this prison spent most of their time standing, since there was no room to sit or lie down. Sometimes, it took prisoners two hours just to get to a bathroom, of which there were few.

Prisoners in these unsanitary conditions have suffered from life-threatening medical and circulatory problems, disease, and hunger. Overcrowding caused 250 to 300 deaths a month before prison conditions improved. Due to a lack of prison space, people accused of taking part in the 1994 violence were often jailed with prisoners accused of minor crimes, such as stealing apples. In addition, more than 300 children suspected of murder were jailed with adults. Aid agencies have worked to improve the situation, but most Rwandan prisons remain overcrowded.

be one of the biggest obstacles to alleviating the conflict in Rwanda. Of the 60,000 people arrested, none had gone to trial by April 1995. As a result, Rwandan prisons were grossly overcrowded and dangerous.

The delay in prosecution was due to a shortage of legal staff, hesitancy by the government to begin trials—possibly out of fear that these trials would fuel more fighting—and lack of money. The former government leaders had fled Rwanda with most of the country's funds. Only 36 judges and 14 prosecutors and assistant prosecutors were available to handle the cases, according to Human Rights Watch/Africa (HRW/A). Only three of these prosecutors had received proper legal training. HRW/A estimated that the Rwandan judicial system needed about 700 judges to operate successfully. The lack of judicial police inspectors posed a problem as well.

There were only 26 inspectors in April 1995, and none of them had cars or resources to travel to crime scenes and carry out investigations. HRW/A estimated that about 750 judicial police inspectors, each with a car, would be required to conduct such investigations.

With the large number of people arrested, overcrowding in the Rwandan prisons became a great concern. International human rights groups recommended that competent lawyers be put into place for trials. They also suggested that the proceedings take place quickly so that prison conditions could improve and innocent citizens could return home. Many observers feared the arrests and hearings would spark more violence. Even if people were found innocent and set free, they were targets for retaliation. NGOs took charge of looking out for the safety and human rights of children who had been arrested for taking part in the violence of 1994. Many of these children were jailed with adults. HRW/A recommended that anyone under the age of 16 be kept in separate jails from adults for safety reasons.

While the Rwandan government was responsible for trying the 60,000 people jailed inside the country, the UN's International Criminal Tribunal for Rwanda was responsible for prosecuting the military and political leaders charged with acts of **genocide** and other human rights abuses. The UN leadership believed that the establishment of the international tribunal would help Rwanda resolve the Hutu-Tutsi conflict and would send the message that such violence was intolerable.

The UN tribunal, located in Tanzania and separate from the Rwandan judicial system, began trying people in November 1995. Initially, however, it didn't function well. Few people were brought to trial, and the court was not successful in prosecuting those believed to have instigated the violence. The process moved slowly, because many members of the former government had fled to countries around the world. HRW/A recommended that countries arrest Rwandans suspected of human rights abuses if they tried to seek exile. In October 1995, HRW/A condemned Kenya's president, Daniel Arap Moi, for allowing Rwandans to seek refuge in Kenya. The group also claimed that Moi had threatened to arrest authorities from Rwanda's international tribunal if they went to Kenya to investigate or arrest Rwandan suspects. But by 1997, Kenya was one of several countries that had

In September 1998, former Rwandan prime minister Jean Kambanda was sentenced to life in prison for the crime of genocide. Kambanda had been prime minister at the height of the violence.

assisted the tribunal by arresting and handing over accused leaders, including Rwanda's interim prime minister, Jean Kambanda, and seven other suspects. Other countries that helped arrest people believed guilty of human rights and genocide crimes were Cameroon, Switzerland, the United States, Zambia, and Belgium.

In early 1997, after receiving more international funding, expanding court facilities, and replacing ineffective personnel, the tribunal began to work more quickly and efficiently. By mid-1997, several cases had gone to trial. In May 1998, Kambanda pleaded guilty to charges of genocide and agreed to testify against others who helped plan the 1994 killings.

The Rwandan judicial system, expanded and better funded, was also making progress. By 1997 the justice department had received substantial foreign assistance and had 910 judges available to try cases. By mid-1997, according to HRW/A, the Rwandan courts had held 142 trials in which 73 people had been found guilty and given prison terms, 61 people had been found guilty

> *"No one is suggesting that every peasant who took a machete should be punished. But those who organized the peasants, who told them to hunt Tutsis and Hutus of the political opposition—the local government officials, the soldiers, the politicians—they must be judged, tried, and punished."*
>
> African Rights

and given death sentences, and 8 people had been declared innocent and set free. Trials continued throughout 1997 and 1998, and on April 24, 1998, the Rwandan government carried out the first executions of those found guilty of participating in the 1994 killings. Despite international criticism, twenty-two people were publicly executed.

The increase in judicial staff was definitely welcomed and necessary, because the Rwandan government has continued to arrest people, mostly Hutus. More than 100,000 prisoners remain in jails throughout the country, and it could take decades to try all those who have been arrested. In addition, international observers have found many flaws in the Rwandan judicial system. A 1998 report by Amnesty International stated that many human rights violations occurred throughout 1997 and 1998 under the Rwandan government. Members of the military and other government personnel have arrested people without having the legal authority to do so. The government often holds these prisoners for long periods without charging them with a crime or giving them a trial. By late 1997, according to HRW/A, about 40 percent of the people in prisons and 80 percent of those being held in other facilities had not been charged with a crime. The delay in prosecution is, in itself, a violation of internationally accepted human rights laws. Rwandan prisoners are also jailed in inhumane conditions—such as extremely overcrowded jails—and suffer from beatings, starvation, and other cruel treatment.

According to several international human rights groups, many of those arrested have received unfair trials. It is not unusual for people accused of genocide-related crimes to go to trial without a defense lawyer, because the government claims it can't afford to provide people with counsel. There also aren't many defense lawyers available, because it is a dangerous job to defend someone accused of genocide or human rights crimes. One lawyer disappeared in 1997, after agreeing to represent genocide suspects. There also have been many reports of people threatening or harming judges and witnesses.

LAND RIGHTS

A major problem for Rwanda since repatriation has been the ongoing struggle among citizens for land rights. Since the civil war ended, approximately 750,000 Tutsi exiles have returned to Rwanda from Uganda, Burundi, Tanzania, and Zaire. Half of the returning Banyarwanda have moved to rural areas in Rwanda, while the other half have settled in towns. In the process, many have confiscated the homes and shops of the Rwandans who had fled the RPF advance. In Kigali, for instance, most of the shops, businesses, and homes were owned by a new community by the summer of 1994. This created a problem when the refugees who were part of the 1994 exodus began to return home. When these Hutu refugees came back to Rwanda in late 1996, they often found that their property had been taken—either by Banyarwanda, RPA soldiers, or people who had stayed behind during the civil war. The new occupants have shown little desire to return the confiscated property.

Under Rwandan law, the original owners have official rights to their properties for up to 10 years after their departure. But when many refugees return home and try to reclaim their properties, the new homeowners often call the authorities and claim that the returning refugees were involved in the 1994 genocide. Whether or not this is true, the returnees are often jailed and sometimes killed. Some returnees attempting to reclaim their property have disappeared. Whole families, including parents, grandparents, children, and even servants, have been taken away and murdered. Out of fear, returning refugees have relocated and left their homes in the possession of the squatters. Some citizens who cannot get back into their homes and

The Politics of Food

By 1998 production of food crops in Rwanda was 88 percent of the pre-war level, which had never been enough to sustain the population. A delay in the rains followed by flooding from excessive rains later in the 1998 season meant that fewer crops were produced that year. Therefore, prices were higher than usual. The excessive rain also caused landslides in some areas, wiping out crops and making it impossible to transport food. Seeds were often unavailable or simply cost too much to buy.

Along with nature, the conflict continues to hamper Rwanda's ability to produce enough food to feed its population. In some areas, such as in the Ruhengeri prefecture, sporadic fighting has temporarily forced Rwandans to move from their farms. When they return, they often find ruined fields, destroyed crops, and looted seed supplies. According to Amnesty International, RPA soldiers have forced Rwandans in the northwest region to cut down their banana plantations because they believe the Hutu rebels will be able to hide in the fields. In other areas, RPA soldiers have ordered Rwandan civilians not to plant crops and to keep the fields open. In some cases, if they do harvest the fields, they are shot by RPA soldiers. Hutu insurgents have also destroyed the fields and crops of farmers they think are sympathetic to the RPA soldiers. In addition, the rebels have demanded food and supplies from civilians and prohibited some Rwandans from selling their harvested food at the markets for fear that the profits might support the government.

As a result, Rwanda has had to rely on limited food donations from foreign organizations. Often the amounts provide just enough sustenance to stay alive. But sporadic fighting has prevented foreign food aid from reaching people in Kibuye, Gisenyi, and Ruhengeri.

A returned Hutu refugee sits outside his home in Kigali while the child of the family occupying the house runs inside. Many returnees found the land and property that they'd left behind confiscated by Tutsi families.

AP/Wide World Photos

don't want to risk negotiations over their properties have moved to different areas of Rwanda. But they often face brutal treatment from their new neighbors.

The Rwandan government has tried to alleviate this situation by setting aside areas for the Banyarwanda to settle. These areas, called resettlement sites, include sections of the once government-protected Akagera National Park in northeastern Rwanda, the town of Byumba in the north, the Kibungo prefecture in southeastern Rwanda, and the region between Gisenyi and Ruhengeri in northwestern Rwanda. Through the Human Rights Field Operation in Rwanda (HRFOR), the UN has as-sisted the Rwandan government in its efforts to return people to their homes. HRFOR observers make sure that the basic human rights of the refugees are not violated at any stage of their return.

THE ROLE OF THE NGOS

NGOs have played a significant role in dealing with the refugee crisis and the post-war situation in Rwanda. Nearly 180 NGOs have worked with Rwandans in Rwanda and neighboring countries to help alleviate disease, get hospitals and clinics up and running, provide food and medicine, build and maintain sanitary

> *"I will tell you the truth . . . The wish for the returnees is that power has to be shared, because the government is dominated by Tutsi and we need some Hutus on our side to be in power, too."*
>
> A Hutu Civilian

living conditions, and provide materials for temporary homes. They also help reunite family members—especially children with their parents or relatives. NGO workers have even helped till the fields, because in many areas there are no citizens to take care of the land and to harvest the crops.

NGO workers have had a significant impact on the communities in which they work. The main health care problem in Rwanda a year after the war was a shortage of medical staff. Many Rwandan doctors and nurses were still living in refugee camps outside of the country.

Working in a War Zone

Aid workers are often faced with daunting challenges and threatening situations when they work in war-torn countries. During the 1994 Rwandan civil war, dozens of aid workers were killed. Others were threatened or bribed, and some had their belongings stolen, even right off their bodies. One NGO's Kigali-based warehouse, a 17-acre space holding food, clothing, and medical equipment, was looted and then destroyed. Aid workers spent two months rebuilding the warehouse and replenishing the supplies.

Sometimes the lack of equipment called for creative solutions. Medical staff at hospitals and clinics had to use whatever equipment they could find. At Mugonero Hospital—located in a closed-down nursing school in northwestern Rwanda—doctors used wooden coat racks to hang up intravenous bags. They reused patient's charts by crossing out the names of former patients to make room for new ones. At the Mugunga refugee camp in Goma, Zaire, aid workers constructed a whole clinic out of makeshift items. The waiting room consisted of wooden planks balanced on large lava rocks. A tarp overhead gave patients protection from the rain. The main area of the clinic contained different tents, each with a separate purpose. There was a dentistry for extractions only, an immunization tent, a pharmacy, an inpatient tent, and several outpatient tents. In another tent, where nurses cared for mothers and children, there was an antique doctor's scale and two homemade devices for measuring a baby's height. The filing cabinet was made out of six metal boxes that were taped together and propped up on cardboard boxes.

Despite inconveniences and threats of violence, most aid workers said the sense of satisfaction and accomplishment made the job worthwhile. "It feels rewarding at the end of the day," said Herb Cruger, a volunteer nurse for Care Australia. "We've done something to help someone's ailments."

An aid worker assists an injured refugee.

Therefore, there wasn't a qualified medical staff in Rwanda to run the clinics and hospitals. Staff was needed to take care of all medical tasks, from treating patients to sorting out paperwork. Medical students were trained to fill these positions, but there was still a high demand for experienced medical staff. To make up for the lack of health care professionals within Rwanda, NGOs spent the year treating victims for disease and war wounds. Within a year after the civil war, the health of the refugees, as well as those living in Rwanda, had improved immensely. The presence of NGOs enabled Rwandans to obtain health care that they might otherwise have gone without.

Aid workers from around the world have brought valuable equipment and skills to Rwandan communities in need. Throughout Rwanda aid workers have worked with local medical staff to help them rebuild clinics and medical facilities. They have also tried to get local residents involved so they can regain a sense of self-worth. At the Mudende clinic in northwestern Rwanda, the staff of the Adventist Development and Relief Agency (ADRA) began asking patients to pay 100 Rwandan francs for treatment. Aid workers felt this would get people used to paying for things again and help them become self-sufficient.

Orphanages have played an important role in postwar Rwanda as well. At the orphanages, Rwandan children have access to medical and dental care. They also receive donated clothing, food, and shelter. And they work on projects, study art, and learn English, French, and Kinyarwanda. The children also have chores to do, such as working in the kitchen and cleaning. They work at jobs around the orphanage that teach them responsibility and self-sufficiency. Children at ADRA's orphanage in Goma were assigned chores

Rwanda's Orphans

Although NGOs have succeeded in reuniting many children with their families, there is still a large number of orphans in Rwanda. The Gakoni orphanage, located about 70 miles northeast of Kigali, houses 166 orphaned and abandoned children in 14 brick-and-clay homes. Each house has a "family" of children with a "mother" to watch over them.

"We mix boys and girls, young and old, together to make it feel like a real family," said Dr. Ranjan Kulasekere, a health worker for the Adventist Development and Relief Agency. "They eat together, pray together, and they have to keep up the house together."

By 9:30 A.M., the children have had breakfast, have washed their clothes, and have cleaned their homes. Then it's off to school, which kids attend in shifts. The youngest attend preschool. Older children go to primary school, where they learn reading, writing, mathematics, and French. All children at the orphanage are required to go to primary school, but only those who pass a test attend secondary school. Otherwise they learn a trade, such as bricklaying or masonry. Some learn agricultural practices. For those who are healthy enough, the remainder of the day is spent playing games and working on agricultural projects. The children grow their own food vegetables and fruits.

and projects. "They work in the kitchen and when we have activities, they have a say in what they do," said Ndayisaba Jean Witcliff, assistant camp manager, in 1994. According to Dr. Ranjan Kulasekere, who oversaw the Gakoni orphanage northeast of Kigali, "Everyone from small to big has to work here. If you don't have money, you have to work. I don't give things for free."

This system, said Kulasekere, gives value to what the children receive. "They don't have to take handouts," he said. "They earned it, and they owe me nothing. It also keeps the kids busy, and they learn a trade. It gives them a sense of satisfaction. There is dignity in work."

NGOs and aid agencies working in Rwanda and its neighboring countries have also created programs to re-unite abandoned children with surviving family members. Sometimes older children and adults have to track down their families on their own. If the NGOs are unable to locate a living relative, they try to place children—who range in age from about four months to 18 years old—in new homes.

LOCAL EFFORTS

While Rwanda needs the help of the international community to heal and rebuild, reconciliation also depends on the efforts of Rwandan citizens. To encourage local efforts, some NGOs are trying to help Rwandan adults help themselves.

The American Refugee Committee (ARC), based in Minneapolis, Minnesota, has been working with refugees and returnees to help them rebuild their lives. Since 1994 ARC has been providing primary health care and training to refugees so that they may become self-reliant. They work together to build health facilities, water systems, and shelters for returnees and displaced persons. ARC is working with the Tumerere Foundation, headed by

Despite the trauma they have suffered, these Rwandan orphans are still able to smile for the camera.

After dinner, children help the "mothers" and aid workers clean up. Then everyone attends a worship service of song and prayer. This may be followed by study hall, if there's electricity, or more playtime. Everyone is in bed by 8:30 P.M.

The American Refugee Committee has played an important role in helping Rwandans get back on their feet, providing medical service (above) *and new housing* (right).

© American Refugee Committee

Rwanda's first lady, Seraphine Bizimungu, to assist widows and children who lost their families in 1994. ARC has already built 250 homes for these people and will continue this rehabilitation project through 1999. Eventually, this and all programs initiated by ARC will be turned over to local people, who will manage and direct the rehabilitation and reconstruction of their country.

A number of locally run organizations are trying to help the Rwandan people cope with the affects of the conflict as well. Avego-Agahozo is a self-help group of Rwandan widows who provide training that will enable other Rwandan widows to find sources of income. Through this training, it is hoped that Rwandan widows will be able to reclaim land, rebuild their lives, and provide for their families. Woman Net is an organization of Rwandan women that helps counsel victims of rape. Duterimbere, one of the largest women's organizations in the country, aids women by providing business loans, legal advice, skills training, home repair, and counseling.

Rwanda and its citizens face many challenges in the years ahead. The country must find a solution to the conflict between Hutus and Tutsis so that the rebuilding process can begin. Unfortunately, no simple solution exists for healing this mountainous country torn apart by ethnic conflict. ⊕

A Rwandan Story

Jean Claude Bizimungu grew up in an affluent, residential neighborhood in Kigali with his parents and seven brothers and sisters. Jean's father owned and operated a successful auto business. The family lived in a big, yellow stone house, with a garage on one side and a chicken coop out back. In December 1993, Jean left his tightly knit family to follow his dreams and go to school in the United States to become a pharmacist.

"My father told me he was very proud of me and to 'Just do it,' " said Jean in 1994. "Every day he would say 'You can do it . . . .' That's the kind of motivation he gave to get me through school."

Jean arrived in Massachusetts unable to speak English. With financial and moral support from his father, he enrolled in English classes at a high school, which he planned to attend for six months before going to college. Four months after he began school, however, the Rwandan civil war started up again. Jean tried calling his family in Kigali, but no one answered the phone. For three months, he was unable to make contact with his family or anyone who might know where they were and if they were safe.

Unable to concentrate on his studies, Jean dropped out of school. The money from his father stopped coming. After three months of uncertainty, Jean learned from a UN peacekeeper in Kigali that a bomb had killed his parents. During the war, the family's house had been caught in the middle of a skirmish between the RPF and FAR. A bomb landed in the middle of the Bizimungu's living room. His brothers and sisters managed to escape through a hole in the fence in their backyard. They traveled about 160 miles on foot until they reached a refugee camp in Bukavu.

After they escaped, a family of Banyarwanda moved into the Bizimungu's house. In November 1994, Jean's brother Paul (above) returned to Kigali and began negotiating with the Tutsi family to buy back his family's home. He also started rebuilding his father's automotive business, which had been damaged during the war. Paul wanted his brothers and sisters to return from Bukavu once everything was in order.

Later that month, Jean and Paul talked on the phone for the first time in eight months. Since it is very expensive to call Rwanda from the United States and a clear telephone connection isn't always available, Jean and Paul spoke on the phone only one more time during the 18 months following their first postwar conversation.

By 1996 Paul was still rebuilding his father's business and fixing up the family's Kigali home, into which his sisters and brothers had moved back. Jean was back at school, studying pharmacology at a small college in Massachusetts and working in the school's financial aid office to help support his studies.

"I have a dream, and that's what's keeping me alive," said Jean. "I'm pushing myself . . . for my father. I miss him so very much."

EPILOGUE*

Although the Rwandan government has stated its commitment to reconciliation, the ethnic conflict continues. In northwestern Rwanda, RPA soldiers have been battling Hutu insurgents bent on overthrowing the government. This conflict has led to numerous human rights abuses by both parties. The Hutu insurgents, seeking to create panic and undermine the government's ability to protect the population, have killed hundreds of civilians for opposing their cause. Most of their victims have been Tutsi civilians and Hutu politicians who are working with the current government. The RPA has responded by killing civilians suspected of collaborating with the insurgents.

At the same time, the Rwandan judicial system and the UN tribunal are continuing their efforts to prosecute individuals who participated in the 1994 violence. However, more than 90 percent of the 120,000 people arrested by the government are still awaiting trials. Many have been in prison since 1994. Because of criticism over the issue of prison overcrowding, the government has started to release elderly and sick individuals.

Despite its commitment to reconciliation in Rwanda, the government has fanned the flames of conflict in the Democratic Republic of the Congo. Rwanda has provided troops and weapons to an insurgency against the government of Laurent Kabila. This rebellion threatens to engulf the whole Great Lakes region in violence.

*Please note: The information presented in *Rwanda: Country Torn Apart* was current at the time of the book's publication. For the most up-to-date information on the conflict, check for articles in the international section of U.S. daily newspapers. *The Economist*, a weekly magazine, is also a good source for up-to-date information. You may also wish to access, via the internet, other sources of information about Rwanda: the Human Rights Watch, at http://www.hrw.org., the Rwanda archive on OneWorld online, at http://www.oneworld.org/news/countries/RW.html, and http://www.inter-media.org., which provides coverage of the International Criminal Tribunal for Rwanda.

CHRONOLOGY

A.D. 1000   Hutu, Tutsi, and Twa peoples establish settled cultures in the Great Lakes region. Farming and cattle raising become primary forms of livelihood.

1400s   Independent Hutu kingdoms begin to expand throughout what would become Rwanda.

1500s   Tutsi monarchy established in central Rwanda. As it expands, the monarchy incorporates smaller Hutu kingdoms.

1600s   Tutsi monarchy is reorganized, and more Hutu kingdoms are incorporated. Rwanda becomes a unified state.

1700s   Tutsi monarchy continues to expand. Tutsi elite establish the ubuhake system.

Early 1800s   Tutsi monarchy expands to include regions in north and south.

1894   Count von Gotzen becomes the first European to explore region of central Africa.

1898   Germany claims modern-day Rwanda and Burundi and incorporates them into German East Africa. The two kingdoms become the territory of Ruanda-Urundi.

1905   Germans mount military expedition against Hutus who refuse to pay royal tribute.

1907   Dr. Richard Kandt named the first governor of Ruanda-Urundi.

1912   German military takes action against rebellious Hutus in the northwest, further strengthening Tutsi dominance. Mwami Musinga pledges loyalty to Germans.

1914   With outbreak of World War I (1914-1918), German and Belgian forces begin battling for territory in Africa.

1916   German forces, facing better equipped British and Belgian troops, withdraw from Ruanda-Urundi. Belgium assumes control of German East Africa.

1924   League of Nations officially hands control of Ruanda-Urundi to Belgium.

1926   Belgians abolish the posts of land chief, cattle chief, and military chief, fusing them into one position.

1928–29   Major famine hits Ruanda-Urundi, leaving 50,000 dead. Belgian administration encourages development of cash and subsistence crops.

1932   Belgian administration institutes new ethnic guidelines. Anyone with 10 or more cows is considered Tutsi, while those with fewer than 10 cows are considered Hutu. Each citizen is given an identification card stating their ethnic identity.

1946   The UN declares Ruanda-Urundi a trust territory and encourages Belgium to make social and political changes to increase the role of the Hutu population.

1952   Belgian administration establishes the Ten-Year Development Plan, which proposes numerous economic, social, and political changes. Belgians also declare that all Rwandan chiefs and subchiefs will be elected, rather than appointed.

1954   Belgian administration abolishes the ubuhake system.

1957   Hutu leaders release the Bahutu Manifesto, which criticizes the political, social, and economic dominance of the Tutsis. Tutsi leaders respond with the Statement of Views, a document that supports the rule of the Tutsis over the Hutus. Tensions between the two groups begin to rise.

1958   Pro-Hutu APROMOSA and PARMEHUTU parties form, followed by the establishment of UNAR, a pro-monarchy, anti-Belgium organization.

1959   Attempts at intimidation by UNAR supporters leads to widespread violence, marking the beginning of the Hutu revolution. Hundreds of Tutsis are killed and thousands driven from their homes. The Belgian administration declares a state of emergency.

1960   First municipal elections in Rwanda are held, with Hutus winning a majority of the seats.

1961   In September a UN-monitored election for national legislative assembly members is held. Hutus again win a majority of seats.

1962   Legislative assembly passes a referendum abolishing the monarchy and establishing the country as a republic. Rwanda becomes independent on July 1, with Grégoire Kayibanda as president.

1963–64   Raids by Tutsi insurgents lead to an anti-Tutsi crackdown by the Rwandan government. Thousands of Tutsis are killed, arrested, or driven out of the country.

1973   Major General Juvénal Habyarimana topples the government of Grégoire Kayibanda in a bloodless military coup.

1975   President Habyarimana eliminates all political parties and forms the MRND party.

1978   Habyarimana establishes a new constitution. Running unopposed, Habyarimana is elected president of Rwanda.

1983   Habyarimana is reelected. Attacks against Banyarwanda in Uganda begin.

1986   National Resistance Army, with support from Tutsi exiles, overthrows government of Milton Obote in Uganda. The RPF begins to organize.

1990   Habyarimana declares his intentions to open up the political process in Rwanda and allow Tutsi exiles to return. In October 7,000 RPF troops invade Rwanda.

1991   Habyarimana signs a new constitution that legalizes political parties and decreases presidential power.

1992   Habyarimana agrees to form a transitional government with members of the opposition. Rwandan government signs a cease-fire with the RPF, but ethnic tension is on the rise. Rwandan army soldiers and Interahamwe members attack Tutsi civilians throughout the country.

1993   The Rwandan government and the RPF sign the Arusha Peace Agreement. Opposition to the accords among pro-Hutu political parties begins to grow and ethnic violence continues.

1994   After meeting with African leaders, President Habyarimana is killed in a plane crash in April. Violence against Tutsis and moderate Hutus begins in Kigali and spreads throughout the countryside. RPF responds to the violence and the civil war resumes. By July, the RPF has defeated the Rwandan Army and ended the violence. But hundreds of thousands of Hutus have fled the country, fearing RPF retaliation. In July and August, refugee situation is at its worst, with thousands dying in refugee camps. By fall the refugee situation has stabilized, but some camps have become bases for Hutu militia members, who begin launching raids in northwestern Rwanda.

1995   UNHCR and African leaders begin efforts to repatriate Rwandan refugees. In November Jimmy Carter forges an agreement with leaders of Uganda, Rwanda, Zaire, and Burundi to speed up the repatriation process. Rwandan government arrests large numbers of Hutus for taking part in the violence of 1994. The UN's International Criminal Tribunal for Rwanda begins trying people accused of genocide and crimes against humanity.

1996   As refugees begin returning to Rwanda, a new conflict erupts in Zaire. A rebel force led by Laurent Kabila begins attacking refugee camps to remove Hutu militia members, whom he believes are aiding the Zairian government. These raids spark a massive movement of refugees back to Rwanda.

1997   As refugees begin to resettle in Rwanda, violence between RPA and Hutu militias continues. UN tribunal and Rwandan judicial system continue holding trials for suspected war criminals.

1998   Rwandan government executes twenty-two people found guilty of taking part in mass killings. Jean Kambanda, the former head of the interim government, is found guilty of genocide.

SELECTED BIBLIOGRAPHY

African Rights. *Death, Despair and Defiance.* London: African Rights, 1995.

Dorsey, Learthen. *Historical Dictionary of Rwanda.* Metuchen, NJ: Scarecrow Press, 1994.

Essack, Karim. *Civil War in Rwanda.* Dar-es-Salaam, Tanzania: Newman Publishing, 1991.

Gourevitch, Phillip. *We Wish to Inform You That Tomorrow We Will Be Killed With Our Families.* New York: Farrar, Strauss & Giroux, 1999.

Keane, Fergal. *Season of Blood.* New York: Viking,

Lemarchand, Rene. *Rwanda and Burundi.* London: Praeger Publishers, 1970.

Pomeray, J.K. *Rwanda: Places and People of the World.* New York: Chelsea House Publishers, 1988.

Prunier, Gérard. *The Rwanda Crisis: History of a Genocide.* New York: Columbia University Press, 1995.

United Nations Department of Public Information. *The United Nations and Rwanda, 1993–1996.* New York: United Nations Department of Public Information, 1996.

INDEX

ABOUT THE AUTHOR

Kari Bodnarchuk is a journalist, editor, and adventurer who has traveled to 30 countries in Africa, Asia, Europe, North America, and the South Pacific. While working as an editor and reporter for a Massachusetts newspaper group, Kari developed and ran a Rwanda relief effort to collect clothing and money for medicines. She traveled to Rwanda in 1994 to report on the distribution of these supplies in refugee camps and hospitals around Rwanda and eastern Zaire. Kari writes for newspapers and magazines and runs classes on adventure travel. She is also the author of Lerner Publications' *Kurdistan: Region under Siege*.

ABOUT THE CONSULTANTS

Andrew Bell-Fialkoff, *World in Conflict* series consultant, is a specialist on nationalism, ethnicity, and ethnic conflict. He is the author of *Ethnic Cleansing*, published by St. Martin's Press in 1996, and has written numerous articles for *Foreign Affairs* and other journals. He is writing a book on the role of migration in the history of the Eurasian Steppe. Mr. Bell-Fialkoff lives in Bradford, Massachusetts.

Timothy Longman is a professor at Vassar College in Poughkeepskie, New York.

SOURCES OF QUOTED MATERIAL

p. 40 Learthen Dorsey, *Historical Dictionary of Rwanda* (Metuchen, NJ: Scarecrow Press, 1994), 9; p. 45, *The United Nations and Rwanda, 1993–1996* (New York: United Nations Department of Public Information, 1996), 8; p. 52 Gerard Prunier, *The Rwanda Crisis: History of a Genocide* (New York: Columbia University Press, 1995), 66; p. 57 United Nations Department of Public Information, *The United Nations and Rwanda, 1993–1996* (New York: United Nations Department of Public Information, 1996), 21; p. 60, Gerard Prunier *The Rwanda Crisis: History of a Genocide* (New York: Columbia University Press, 1995), 166; p. 67 "Rwanda Rebels Urge Refugees to Halt Flight," *Los Angeles Times*, 20 July, 1994, A1; p. 71 "Running Scared," *Newsweek*, 25 November, 1996, 40; p. 72 excerpt from a speech given by President Pasteur Bizimungu, 5 September, 1995. Quoted in "Rwanda and Burundi—A Report," on the Amnesty International Website, http://www.amnesty.org.uk/reports/rwa_bur/6.html; p. 73 Human Rights Watch Arms Project, "Rwanda/Zaire Rearming with Impunity: International Support for the Perpetrators of the Rwandan Genocide," *Human Rights Watch*, vol. 7, no. 4 (May 1995); p. 82 African Rights, *Rwanda: Death, Despair, and Defiance* (London: African Rights, 1995), 1175; p. 84 "Rwanda's Past Again Vies to Be Prologue," *New York Times*, 24 November, 1996; p. 85; p. 86 "Makeshift Clinics Tend to 1000s," *The Middlesex News*, 9 December, 1994, 1A; p. 86 excerpt from the author's interview with Dr. Ranjan Kulasekere, December 1994; p. 87 ibid.; p. 87 ibid; p. 89 excerpt from the author's interview with Jean Claude Bizimungu, October 1994; p. 89 ibid.